Adobe Photoshop
2024 Beginner's Guide

A Detailed Step-By-Step Tutorial with Useful Tips & Tricks for
Photographers to Master All the New Features in Adobe
Lightroom Classic 2024

Ernest
Woodruff

Table of Contents

INTRODUCTION

Adobe has released the most recent version of its widely used photo editing and management program, and it is called Adobe Lightroom Classic 2024. It caters to photographers of all skill levels, from amateurs to seasoned experts, by providing a comprehensive assortment of features.

The new tools that are included in Lightroom Classic 2024 will make the process of editing your images simpler and more time-effective. For instance, the object selection function, which is driven by AI, will make it much simpler for you to make exact adjustments to certain things in the photos you have taken. This will not only save you time and work but will also enable you to generate photos that have a more finished and expert appearance.

Your photo editing tasks will become easier as a result of Lightroom Classic 2024's enhanced performance, which will save you time. Lightroom Classic is already a very responsive and quick-moving piece of software; however, the new speed changes will make it much more so. This implies that you will be able to edit your images in a way that is both quicker and more effective.

Continue reading to learn more about the new Adobe Lightroom Classic 2024.

CHAPTER ONE

New Features of Adobe Photoshop Lightroom Classic 2024

Adobe has announced the following new features that will be included in Lightroom Classic 2024:

- **Object selection made easier with AI**: Adobe Lightroom Classic 2024 will make it easier to select objects in photos by using artificial intelligence in the process. Since this is the case, users will no longer need to manually mask individual items to make exact adjustments to those objects.

- **Enhanced performance**: Compared to earlier versions, Lightroom Classic 2024 will have a quicker processing speed and a better response time. This comes as a result of a variety of performance enhancements, one of which is a whole new rendering engine that is GPU-accelerated.

- **Brand new presets and brushes**: Adobe Lightroom Classic 2024 will come with a brand new collection of presets and brushes, which will make it easier for users to produce great photographs.

- **Additional new features**: Lightroom Classic 2024 will also contain several additional new capabilities, including the capability to edit HDR photos, build custom color profiles, and export photos to a range of various formats.

More features:

- **Accelerate image-editing with GPU support**

Enhance the experience of picture editing by using the graphics processing unit (GPU) of your machine.

- **Organize your collections with color labels**

Labels of any color can be assigned to collections, collection sets, and smart collections respectively.

- **Assistance with newly released imaging cameras and lenses**

Support has been added for a variety of new camera and lens profiles.

- **Additional improvements**

Learn more about the PNG export, batch merge for HDR and panoramas, and other new features included in this edition by reading the accompanying documentation.

How to download and Install Lightroom Classic 2024

The following is a list of the minimal system requirements needed to run Adobe Lightroom Classic 2024:

- **Operating system** requirements include Windows 10 (64-bit) version 21H2 or later, as well as macOS Monterey (version 12.0 or later).

- The CPU can be either an Intel Core i5 processor or an AMD Ryzen 5 processor.

- **Memory**: 8 gigabytes of random-access memory (RAM); we suggest 16 gigabytes or more.

- **Hard disk space:** 10 GB of accessible storage space on the hard disk (extra free space is necessary during installation and sync)

- **Display a resolution** of 1280 pixels by 768 pixels (1280 pixels by 1920 pixels or higher is preferred) on the monitor.

Here are the steps:

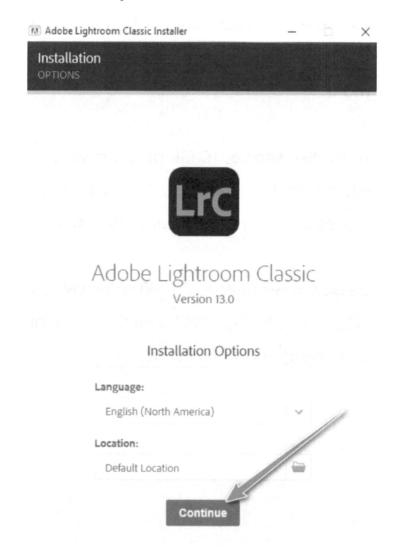

The following is an in-depth walkthrough that will teach you how to download and install Lightroom Classic:

You will need a current membership to Adobe Creative Cloud to be able to download and install Lightroom Classic. You can create an account on the Adobe website if you do not already have one.

- To get started, go to Adobe's official website and sign in using your Adobe ID.

- Select "**Creative Cloud**".

- To download the installer for Creative Cloud, you will need to click the "**Download**" option.

- Find the file that was downloaded for the installation, and then start it.

- To finish installing Adobe Creative Cloud on your computer, you will need to follow the instructions that appear on-screen.

- Activate the Adobe Creative Cloud program on your device.

- Use the Adobe ID you created together with your password to sign in.

- Locate the "**Apps**" tab inside the Creative Cloud program that you are using.

- Search for "**Lightroom Classic**" in the list of programs that are accessible to you.

- To install Lightroom Classic, click the "**Install**" button that is located next to the program.

- Lightroom Classic will be downloaded and installed on your computer automatically by the Creative Cloud app.

- Once the installation has been finished, you will be able to use Lightroom Classic using the

Creative Cloud app or through the apps or programs menu on your computer.

- You may be prompted to sign in with your Adobe ID once again the first time you run Lightroom Classic for the first time.

- To activate and configure Lightroom Classic, follow any further instructions that may appear on the screen.

- Conducting frequent checks to see whether there have been any changes is a recommended best practice. *(NB: **Adobe regularly rolls out updates designed to enhance speed and offer new capabilities**).*

- In the Creative Cloud app, choose the "**Updates**" tab to determine whether or not there are any new versions of Lightroom Classic that have been released.

How Should I Use Lightroom Classic in These Various Situations?

Lightroom Classic's applicability extends to a wide range of situations, including the following:

- **Photography as a profession**: Lightroom Classic is the image editing software that the majority of professional photographers like to use. It provides a broad variety of tools and functions that are necessary for professional photography, such as color grading, lens corrections, and batch editing, amongst others.

- **Photography as a hobby**: Lightroom Classic is another excellent choice for those interested in photography as a hobby. Even if you don't have a lot of expertise, you can easily edit and organize your photos with the help of the app's many functions since they make it so simple.

- **Photography for social media platforms**: You can use Lightroom Classic to edit and publish your photos on various social media platforms. It provides several distinct export options that are tailored to the requirements of various social networking networks.

Why use Adobe Photoshop Lightroom Classic 2024?

Adobe Photoshop Lightroom Classic is a robust and extensively used software solution that was developed specifically for digital image experts and professional photographers. It offers a complete solution for the management, editing, and organization of enormous quantities of digital pictures. Even if certain features could have been updated in the 2024 version, the fundamental capabilities and explanations for why people use

Lightroom Classic are likely to continue to be relevant.

The following is a list of strong arguments in favor of using Adobe Photoshop Lightroom Classic:

- **Non-destructive Editing**: This editing method is known as "**non-destructive**." This ensures that the original versions of your photos are not altered in any way, while the metadata is updated to reflect any changes you make. Because of this, you won't have to worry about accidentally destroying your original files if you want to try out a new editing technique.

- **Efficient Organization**: The program offers a comprehensive set of tools for arranging and managing the contents of your picture collection. You can quickly find certain photos by creating collections, applying keywords to them, and using the many available filters. This is very helpful for photographers who work with a large number of photographs.

- **RAW Editing**: Lightroom Classic performs very well when processing RAW files, giving photographers a great deal of control over picture parameters such as exposure, white balance, and sharpness. Having the capability to work directly with RAW data guarantees the finest possible output quality.

- **Integrated Workflow:** Lightroom Classic connects itself without any hiccups into the larger ecosystem that is Adobe Creative Cloud. When you need to do more complex editing operations, such as in Photoshop, you can transition between Lightroom and other Adobe products with ease. The post-processing procedure is made more efficient as a result of this integrated workflow.

- **Presets and Profiles**: Lightroom Classic comes with a variety of different presets and profiles, which enable users to quickly apply a variety of different appearances or styles to their photographs with just the click of a button. Additionally, you can build and store your own presets, which enables you to maintain a uniform visual style across several photos.

- **Tools for sophisticated Editing**: Although it does not have as many features as Adobe Photoshop, Lightroom Classic does provide a set of sophisticated editing tools. These tools include spot healing, adjustment brushes, gradient and radial filters, and gradient and radial gradients. These tools make it possible to make fine-grained modifications to certain parts of a picture.

- **Cloud Synchronization**: Lightroom Classic now enables you to synchronize your picture collection and adjustments across numerous devices thanks to the integration of Adobe Creative Cloud. Because of this, you will be able to continue working on your photographs regardless of where you are located without losing any progress.

- **Map Module**: Lightroom Classic is equipped with a Map module that not only enables you to geotag your photos but also provides a graphical depiction of the location where the photographs were shot. This is especially helpful for photography that is centered on travel or a specific area.

- **Printing and Exporting:** Lightroom Classic is equipped with strong features that allow users to print their photos and export them in a variety of file formats. Lightroom Classic gives you a lot of options when it comes to exporting your work, so you can get high-resolution photographs for printing or copies optimized for the web.

- **Updates & Support**: Adobe often provides updates to enhance performance, offer new features, and fix any problems that may arise. In addition, the program is maintained by a large community of users, which makes it simpler to get online lessons, suggestions, and help.

Differences between Lightroom and Lightroom Classic

There was a time when Lightroom was the only program available. However, ever since Adobe shifted to cloud-based and subscription-based services, Lightroom has had two iterations: Lightroom Classic and Lightroom (formerly known as Lightroom CC, where CC stands for "Creative Cloud"). Lightroom Classic is the more traditional version. Lightroom Classic is a version of Lightroom that can only be used on a desktop computer. In contrast, Lightroom is a cloud-based editing service that saves the original versions of your photographs in Adobe's cloud.

There is a possibility that you will be able to download both Lightroom Classic and Lightroom after purchasing from Adobe; however, this is dependent on the specific package that you choose. However, this does not imply that you should make use of both of them simultaneously. Even though they have certain similarities, these two apps couldn't be more dissimilar to one another.

The Struggle with Naming

Lightroom Classic and Lightroom have been products that Adobe has sold to customers for several years. Originally, the main distinction between the two was that Lightroom Classic was a stand-alone software with a perpetual license, and Lightroom was a component of the subscription model used by Adobe's Creative Cloud. Over time, Adobe began to separate them from one another and add distinctive characteristics to each one.

The user interface of Lightroom Classic is identical to the one seen in earlier versions of Lightroom that were distributed under a perpetual license. Lightroom, on the other hand, has its unique characteristics. It has a streamlined and less powerful interface, but it is cross-platform, which means that you can edit your photographs on your desktop computer and then continue working on them on your mobile device or tablet.

To summarize it all:

- Lightroom Classic is the latest version of Adobe's widely used RAW editing program for desktop computers.
- Lightroom is an editor that can be used on several platforms and is hosted in the cloud. However, compared to Lightroom Classic, it includes fewer editing and organizing options.

Examining the Differences and Similarities Between the New Lightroom Products

If there's anything you've been able to accomplish in previous versions of Lightroom, you can do it in Lightroom Classic as well. In other words, Lightroom Classic lives up to its name and is "**classic**." It is also more complex and has superior features linked to organizing; the only notable exception is that it does not have the artificial intelligence keyboarding that Lightroom has.

Lightroom, on the other hand, has a relatively straightforward interface. It is possible to edit the same picture on your desktop computer, laptop computer, tablet computer, and mobile phone, so you do not have to bother about moving photographs between devices. It also does not have a steep learning curve, which means that the vast majority of individuals should have no trouble understanding what is going on. On the other hand, it is not as sophisticated as Lightroom Classic, and if you want to take advantage of the unique capabilities that it has to offer in comparison to Lightroom Classic, you will need to pay Adobe to keep your photographs in the cloud. If you have terabytes upon terabytes of images, this may get rather pricey.

Even while Lightroom Classic has more sophisticated editing options, the majority of the useful ones have also been included in Lightroom. This includes elements such as local modifications, which are essential for more complex editing, for example. Lightroom also features a function that uses artificial intelligence to search for keywords, which is a handy method to identify a collection of photographs that all pertain to the same subject.

Who Should Use Lightroom Classic?

Do you consider yourself an advanced photographer or a professional? Have you worked with Adobe Lightroom in the past at any point? If this is the case, Lightroom Classic is the best option for your job.

Tethering, soft proofing, and complicated organization are just some of the additional capabilities that are available to satisfy the needs of expert photographers. The artificial intelligence keyword search that Lightroom offers may be rather pleasant, but the majority of pros will be more concerned with other aspects of the program, such as the availability of plugins, numerous catalogs, fully-fledged develop tools, and so on. Lightroom Classic is designed to compete in the same market space as its predecessors.

The users should include:

- Photographers with advanced skills or professional experience who are familiar with Lightroom and value the breadth and depth of its feature set.

- Photographers who edit a huge number of images, the storage of which would either be prohibitively costly if done in the cloud or impractical if done via a slower internet connection.

- Photographers who use plugins developed by a third party.

Who Should Use Lightroom?

When compared to Lightroom Classic, the newer version, Lightroom, might give the impression of being somewhat simplified. It lacks a number of the elements that photographers regard to be either essential or even required for their work in a professional capacity. Nevertheless, in a lot of ways, this is one of the most significant advantages of using Lightroom. Photographers who place a higher priority on intuitive operation in their program than on an extensive feature set and powerful capabilities are ideal candidates for using Lightroom.

Lightroom is designed with the end user in mind and has a feature set that is geared at making the learning curve as shallow as possible. Despite this, it is still capable of quite complex levels of editing and organizing. As a result, it is the superior program for those who engage in hobbies, particularly those who have numerous devices, such as a desktop, a laptop, and a tablet, which they often move between.

Does this imply that more experienced photographers will never make use of Lightroom? For instance, if you conduct a lot of social media marketing, you'll want the flexibility to edit films on the fly (i.e., smartphone recordings of behind-the-scenes action). That is possible with Lightroom, but not with Lightroom Classic.

In a nutshell, Lightroom was designed to be used on mobile devices in addition to its utility as a photographic program for amateurs. Lightroom Classic makes more sense if you are an accomplished photographer who does not use your mobile device as a vital element of your brand and marketing plan.

The people who should use it include:

- Photographers who take pictures on occasion or as a pastime and are looking for a post-processing program that is simple to use yet surprisingly strong and compatible with numerous platforms.

- Working professionals who maintain an active presence on social media platforms like YouTube and often produce and post material while on the go, mostly using their devices.

- Photographers who want to edit their work on numerous devices simultaneously without having to worry about managing their files

CHAPTER TWO

Understanding Lightroom Classic

Interface

How to create a custom workspace

In Adobe Lightroom Classic, you can create a customized workspace by setting up panels, tools, and modules according to your workflow.

Here are the steps:

- Launch Adobe Lightroom Classic.

- Locate the module you want to change by navigating to it. Lightroom Classic has the following modules: Develop, Map, Book, Slideshow, Print, and Web.

Adjust the Tools and Panels

- **Panels**: You have panels with a variety of tools and settings on the sides of the screen. Click the tiny triangle at the top of each panel to collapse or expand it to help you order these panels. Panels can be dragged around to suit your preferences.

- **Solo Mode:** To enter Solo Mode, right-click on the header of a panel and choose "**Solo Mode**." This makes the workplace clearer by automatically collapsing all other panels.

- **Toolbar**: The toolbar is often seen at the screen's bottom. You may pick which tools to show by doing a right-click on it. By doing this, you can simplify the toolbar by adding just the tools that you use the most often.

Create and Save a Workspace

- **Arrange the Windows:** To make the most of your workspace, move and resize the various windows within the module.

- **Window Menu:** Select **Window > Workspaces** from the menu bar. One has the option to choose among pre-existing workspaces such as **"Default," "Develop," or "Slideshow,"** or to establish a new workspace.

- **New Workspace**: Select "**Save Current As New Workspace**" to establish a new workspace. Give your workspace a name.

Apply the Custom Workspace

- **Switch Between Workspaces**: To switch between workspaces, pick the appropriate workspace by heading to **Window > Workspaces**.

- **Reset to Default**: Select **Window > Workspaces > Reset to Default Workspace** to return to the original workspace.

Maintain your customized workspace's adjustments in light of your changing workload. These procedures can be repeated as many as necessary to make modifications.

How to understand file types and formats

Understanding File Types:

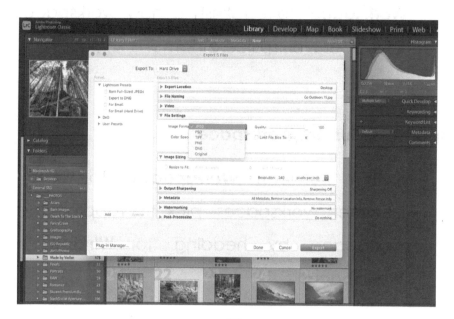

Understanding the many file formats supported by Adobe Lightroom Classic is essential for effective picture management and editing.

RAW Files:

- Unprocessed data straight from the camera's sensor is included in RAW files.

- They provide more post-processing flexibility, enabling quality-preserving tweaks like exposure and white balance.

- The file extensions.NEF (Nikon),.CR2 (Canon), and.ARW (Sony) are often used for RAW files.

Digital Negative (DNG):

- Adobe's RAW file open standard is intended to serve as a global RAW format.

- DNG files contribute to long-term compatibility and are often smaller than proprietary RAW files.

Joint Photographic Experts Group (or JPEG):

- Since JPEG files are smaller in size and are compressed, they are often used for sharing images.

- Due to their lossy format, some picture data is lost during the compression process.

Tagged Image File Format (TIFF):

- TIFF files preserve excellent picture quality since they are uncompressed.

- Due to the lossless compression, it is appropriate for printing and preservation.

Understanding Formats:

Library Module:

- To manage and arrange your picture collection, use the Library section.

- The catalog file (.lrcat) in Adobe Lightroom Classic contains information about your photographs.

Develop Module:

- You can change your images in a non-destructive manner using the Develop module.

- Lightroom allows for the storage of edits as metadata while maintaining the original picture.

Exporting Files:

- Select the right file format for your intended usage when exporting photos.

- While TIFF or PSD (Photoshop Document) can be used for high-quality printing, JPEG is often shared online.

Importing Files:

- When importing images, you have the option to transfer them to a designated folder and, if you'd like, convert them to Adobe DNG format.

- Use ratings, flags, and keywords to arrange your imported files.

Keywords and Metadata:

- To facilitate picture searches, use metadata to provide elements like keywords, captions, and copyright information.

Presets:

- Create presets in Lightroom to save time during post-processing by applying parameters to one or more photographs.

Catalog and Backup Management:

- To avoid data loss, regularly back up your Lightroom library.

- If you want improved performance, think about optimizing and cleaning up your inventory.

Understand the Library Module

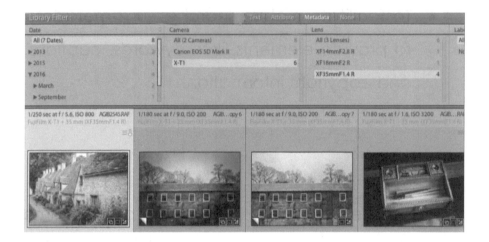

Importing and Organizing:

Importing Photos:

- To import images from external devices or folders into your Lightroom library, use the Import dialog.

- During the import procedure, apply metadata, and keywords, and develop settings.

Organizing with Folders:

- See and organize your pictures in a hierarchy based on folders.

- Make folders, move them, or rename them to organize your picture collection.

Grid View:

Thumbnail Grid:

- By default, the Grid View is shown by the Library Module, which shows a grid of thumbnail images.

- Mark and arrange photos with flags, stars, and colored labels.

Sorting & Filtering:

- Apply different filters to refine your picture selection according to characteristics such as ratings, flags, and metadata.

- Arrange photos in a custom order, by file name, or by capture time.

Loupe View:

Detailed View:

- Use the Loupe View to enlarge individual photographs for a closer look.

- Assess the clarity and features of the picture.

Compare and Survey Views:

Comparing Images:

- To choose the best picture, compare many shots side by side.

- To further refine your decision, use the Survey View.

Metadata and Keywording:

Adding Keywords:

- Give photos keywords to help with effective classification and search.

- To achieve more precise organization, use a hierarchical keyword structure.

Metadata Panel:

- Examine and modify metadata data, including location, camera settings, and copyright.

- Use metadata presets to make quick edits.

Collections:

Collecting and Organizing:

- To organize relevant photos together without changing the folder structure, use collections.

- Smart Collections change dynamically following preset standards.

Quick Develop

Basic Edits:

- Use the Library Module to quickly alter color, contrast, and exposure.

- Perfect for quick modifications without having to open the Develop Module.

Publish Services:

Online Sharing:

- Upload images straight to websites such as Behance or Adobe Portfolio.

- Simplify the sharing of your work procedure.

Synchronize and Backup

Sync Editing:

- Sync changes and information among several photos.

- For data protection, make backups of your catalog.

How to activate and use Solo Mode

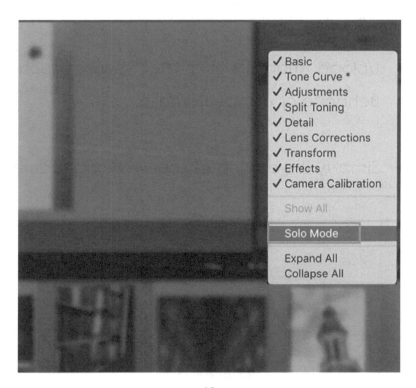

Activate Adobe Lightroom Classic's Solo Mode:

- Launch Adobe Lightroom Classic 2024.

- Locate and choose the "**Library**" module at the top of the screen in Lightroom Classic.

- The Collections panel is located on the Library module's left side. To make it larger, click the "**Collections**" option.

- You can see the contents of a single collection at a time using the "**Solo Mode**" function, which makes it simpler to concentrate on certain groups of images.

- In the Collections panel, right-click on any collection.

- From the context menu that opens, look for an option that looks like "**Solo Mode**" or "**Activate Solo Mode**." Selecting it will initiate Solo Mode.

How to Use Adobe Lightroom Classic's Solo

Mode

Once Solo Mode is enabled, you can use its functions to optimize your workflow:

- You can now work with specific collections without being distracted by other collections while Solo Mode is enabled.

- To see and modify photos within a particular collection, go through your collections.

- In the Collections panel, click on the chosen collection to swap between them.

- Solo Mode can be disabled if you want to see the contents of numerous collections at once.

- In the Collections panel, right-click on any collection to bring up an option labeled

"**Deactivate Solo Mode**" or something similar. To disable Solo Mode, click on it.

- When working on arranging and modifying photos in a specific collection, use Solo Mode. If you want to organize your process and have a big library, this might be useful.

Understanding the Develop Module

A great tool for photographers to organize, edit, and improve their images is Adobe Lightroom Classic. Lightroom's Develop Module, which offers sophisticated capabilities for picture editing and enhancement, is an essential component.

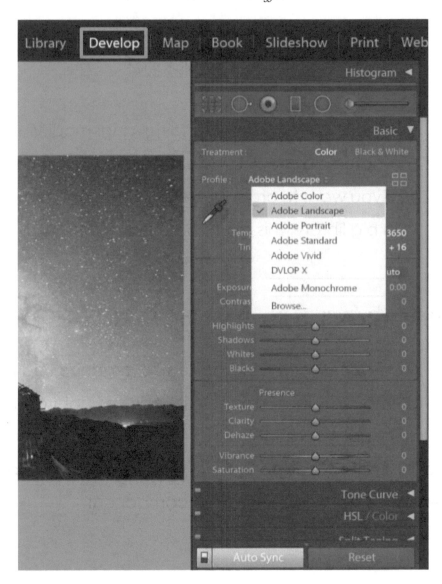

The steps:

- Launch Adobe Lightroom Classic 2024.

- Use the "**D**" key or the "Develop" tab located in the upper right corner to get to the "**Develop**" module.

Workspace Overview:

There are many panels in the Develop Module, each with a distinct function.

- **Basic Panel:** Modify exposure, contrast, and white balance, among other fundamental settings.

- **Tone Curve Panel**: Use curves to fine-tune tonal adjustments.

- **HSL/Color Panel**: For fine-grained color customization, adjust each color channel.

- **Detail Panel**: Tools for noise reduction and sharpening.

- **Lens Corrections Panel**: Adjust chromatic aberration and lens distortions.

- **Effects Panel**: Add grain and post-crop vignetting.

- **Camera Calibration Panel**: Fine-tune color profiles using the camera calibration panel.

Basic Panel:

- **Exposure**: Modify the brightness overall.

- **Contrast**: Manage the distinction between bright and dark areas.

- **Tones**: Adjust highlights, shadows, whites, and blacks.

- **Temperature/Tint**: Modify the hue equilibrium.

Tone Curve Panel:

- To precisely change the tone, use the curve.

- Make individual adjustments to the highlights, lights, darks, and shadows.

HSL/Color Panel:

- Adjust each color channel's hue, saturation, and luminance separately.

- Set aside certain colors to be adjusted.

Detail Panel:

- **Sharpening**: Boost the details in the picture.

- **Noise Reduction**: Reduce picture noise.

Lens Corrections Panel:

- Automatically adjust for chromatic aberration and lens distortion.

- If necessary, manually correct chromatic aberration, vignetting, and distortion.

Effects Panel:

- **Post-crop Vignetting**: Adjust the image's edge brightness or darkness.

- **Grain**: For aesthetic purposes, add a film-like texture.

Camera Calibration Panel:

- Modify the profile to optimize the depiction of color.

Before and After Views:

- Toggle between the original and modified views by using the "**Y**" key.

- Analyze various editing phases using "**Before/After**" views.

CHAPTER THREE

How to Understand the Lightroom

Classic Catalog System

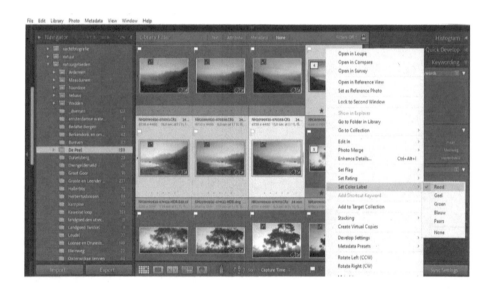

How to set up your catalog

Creating a catalog, importing photos, and sorting them into folders are the three steps involved in setting up your catalog in Adobe Lightroom Classic.

Here are the steps:

- The first step is to open and install Adobe Lightroom Classic. Check to ensure that you have the classic version of Adobe Lightroom installed on your computer.

- In the Library module, choose the **File menu** from the available options.

- Make sure you choose "**New Catalog**."

- Decide where on your computer you would want to save the catalog files, and then choose that place.

- Give your catalog a name that has some kind of significance.

- You will need to choose the parameters for your catalog, which include the kind of previews as well as the metadata settings.

- You can modify these parameters following the preferences you have established for your process.

- Once you have customized the settings to your liking, use the "**Create**" option.

Import Photos

- In the upper right corner of the screen, choose the Library module to open it.

- If your photos are stored on a memory card or an external disk, you will need to connect those devices to your computer.

- Within the Library module, go to the bottom-left corner and choose the "**Import**" button.

- Choose the origin of your images, which might be your camera, an external disk, or another device.

- Select the location where the images will be copied, the naming conventions for the files, and the metadata settings.

- To import the photos into your catalog, you will need to click the "**Import**" option.

Organize your Catalog

- Within the Library module, you can quickly make your photographs searchable by adding relevant keywords to them.

- To arrange photos that are connected, you should use collections. In the Collections panel, clicking on the plus sign ('+') will allow you to create a new collection.

- For improved organizing, you should add information to each of your photos, such as captions, titles, and ratings.

- Mark the images you consider to be your greatest work and give them star ratings to help you choose your favorites.

Back up your Catalog

- Navigate to the Catalog Settings section of the Library module by selecting **Edit > Catalog Settings**.

- Make sure the "**Backup**" option is turned on, and then choose how often you want backups to be created automatically.

- It is recommended that you manually back up your catalog regularly by selecting "**Back Up Catalog**" from the File menu.

Export and Share:

Export Images:

- Navigate to the Library section of the app and choose the pictures you want to export.

- To customize the export options, go to the "**File**" menu, choose "**Export**," and then select "**Configure**."

Share Online:

- You can either export your photos from Lightroom so that you can share them on other platforms, or you can share your photos straight from Lightroom to social media.

How to upgrade a catalog from a previous version

Backup your Catalog

To avoid any loss of data during the upgrade process, it is essential to first create a backup of your current catalog. To do this:

- Launch **Adobe Lightroom Classic 2024.**

- To export the catalog, go to the "**File**" menu and choose "**Export as Catalog.**"

- Before clicking "**Save**," choose a place on your computer to save the backup catalog, then click "**Save.**"

- Ensure that the backup contains both the previews and the negatives, which are the original photos.

Update to the recent version of Adobe Lightroom Classic

Check to see that the most recent version of Adobe Lightroom Classic is installed on your computer. You can check to see if there are any updates available by heading to the "Help" menu and choosing "**Updates**." To install any available updates, just follow the instructions that appear on-screen.

Open Lightroom Classic and click "Initiate Upgrade"

- Proceed to launch the Adobe Lightroom Classic application.

- A notification will appear in the form of a dialog box if the program determines that your catalog is outdated and needs to be updated. Ensure you select **Upgrade.**

- Lightroom will ask you for your approval before upgrading the catalog. Since the update is not reversible, you should make sure that you have previously backed up your catalog.

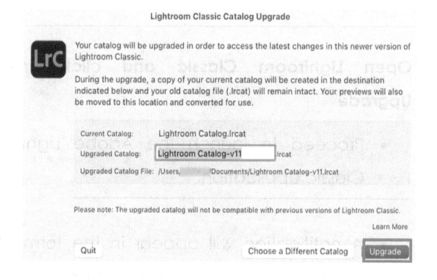

- The process of upgrading may take some time, depending on the size of your catalog, so please be patient. Lightroom will show a progress meter, and you shouldn't stop the process at any point while it's running.

- When the upgrading process is finished, Lightroom will launch with the improved version of your library. Make sure that all of your photographs, their information, and the modifications you've made are still there.

- Once the upgrade has been completed without incident, you should think about removing any prior previews to clear some space on your hard disk. To delete all preview data, go to the "**Catalog Settings**" menu option (**File > Catalog Settings**) and choose the "**General**" tab before clicking the "**Delete All Preview Data**" button.

- You have the option of optimizing the catalog if you want to further increase its speed. Follow the on-screen instructions after selecting "**Optimize Catalog**" from the "**File**" menu.

How to export and delete a catalog

Exporting a Catalog:

- Launch Adobe Lightroom Classic 2024, and when it has loaded, make sure you are in the Library module.

- While in the Library module, access the module's menu and choose **'File**.'

- Under the **'File'** menu, choose the option to **'Export as Catalog**.'

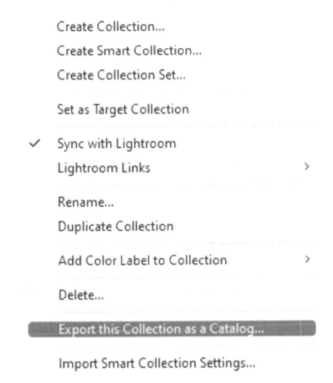

- A modal window will pop up, allowing you to choose the directory in which the exported catalog will be saved when it has been created. *(NB: Pick a location for the catalog's destination folder, and give it a name).*

- Choose whatever export settings you want to use for the file. You have the option to include negative file types, construct previews, and integrate any accessible previews.

- To create the exported catalog, choose the **'Export'** option from the menu.

Deleting a Catalog:

- Before you delete a catalog, verify that you either have a backup copy of the catalog or that you have exported it, as was covered before.

- If Adobe Lightroom Classic is currently running, exit the app.

- Move the cursor to the directory in which your Lightroom catalog is kept and click there. On most computers, the Pictures folder is the place that is selected automatically as the default.

- Locate the file in the catalog that has the extension ".lrcat." The catalog that you view inside Lightroom will be the same name as the file that you save from it.

- When you have found the catalog file, you have the option to either drag it to the trash or recycling bin or right-click on it and pick the **'Delete'** option.

- If asked, confirm the deletion of the item.

Before you delete anything, ensure sure you have a recent copy saved somewhere else. When you delete a catalog, the references to your photographs and modifications are removed, so make sure you have copies of everything just in case you delete anything important.

How to move catalogs to a new location

In most cases, the following actions need to be taken to move catalogs in Adobe Lightroom Classic:

- It is very important to establish a copy of your Lightroom catalog before making any changes to it. If anything goes wrong during the relocation, you will still have a duplicate of your catalog thanks to this precaution.

- Before beginning the procedure, be sure that Adobe Lightroom Classic has been closed from the app screen.

- The third step is to identify the location of your current Lightroom catalog. This location stores your catalog file, which has the extension.lrcat. On Windows, the Pictures folder is often the default position, whereas on macOS, the Pictures directory that is included inside your user folder is the usual location.

- Either copy or transfer the complete folder that contains your catalog file to the new place. It's possible that this is a separate disk or folder on your computer, or it might even be an external storage device.

- Lightroom may not be able to find your photos if you've relocated your catalog to a new disk or folder. In this case, you'll need to update the folder paths. When you resume Lightroom, you can see a message asking you to find any folders that are missing. Lightroom will automatically update the paths after you have navigated to the new location of your photos.

- If the software does not automatically detect the new position of your catalog, you can open it manually by going to **File > Open Catalog** and choosing the catalog file in its new place. This can be done if the program does not immediately identify the new location of your catalog.

- Verify the Changes Perform a second check in the new place to ensure that all of your photographs, modifications, and metadata have been preserved. Check to verify that Lightroom is operating properly with the new catalog location.

- Once you have verified that everything is functioning as it should in the new place, you have the option of deleting the old catalog files in the prior location to make more storage space.

How to copy keywords to a new catalog

The steps:

- The first step is to launch Lightroom Classic 2024 on your PC.

- Launch the catalog from which you want to copy the keywords, and have it open in a new tab.

- You can access the Library module by either using the "**G**" key on your keyboard or clicking on the icon that represents the Library module that is located in the upper right.

- Choose the pictures that include the terms that you want to copy and paste. To move among your photos, you can either use the Filmstrip at the bottom of the screen or the Grid view by using the "**G**" key.

- After you have chosen which photographs to use, right-click on any one of those images, and then select "**Metadata**" from the context menu that appears. After that, click the option to "**Copy Metadata**."

- Make sure you are in the new catalog that you are going to copy the keywords into.

- Find the photos in the new catalog that you wish to apply the copied keywords to, and then pick those images.

- Use the right mouse button to choose one of the photographs in the newly created catalog, then select "**Metadata**" from the context menu, and finally choose "**Paste Metadata**."

- A confirmation dialog box may pop up after you make modifications. Make sure that the box labeled "**Keywords**" is checked, and then either click "**OK**" or "**Paste**."

- Examine each of the pictures in the new catalog to check and see whether the keywords were correctly carried over.

- Remember to save your changes to the new catalog before you go any further.

How to use select object

Here are the steps:

- On your computer, start Adobe Lightroom Classic. Make sure that the most recent version is installed so that you can take advantage of any new features or enhancements.

- You will need to import your photos if they are not already in the library of your Lightroom program. To import your photographs into Lightroom, go to the "**Library**" module and click on the "**Import**" option there.

- The "**Select**" tool is commonly used in the "Develop" module, which is where you can make edits to your images. Simply go to the top-right-hand area of the user interface and choose the "**Develop**" module.

- In the filmstrip that appears at the bottom of the screen, click on the image that corresponds to the photo that you want to work on.

- The "**Select**" tool can be found in the toolbar on the right side of the screen. The icon itself and its placement may be different, but most of the time, it'll be represented by a cursor or some kind of selection tool.

- Depending on the version of Lightroom Classic that you are using, you may have access to a variety of different choices for selecting items. This may include a brush tool, which would allow for freehand selections; a gradient tool, which would allow for linear choices; or a radial tool, which would allow for circular selections. Determine which tool will best serve your purposes and go from there.

- To create your selection, click and drag the selection tool over the region that has to be adjusted. You can paint over the precise areas of the image that you wish to have included in the selection if you are using the brush tool.

- After you have made your first pick, you can decide to further refine it. To fine-tune the selection, look for choices such as feathering, which reduces the sharpness of the edges of your selection, as well as additional adjustment sliders.

- Now that you've made your decision, you can begin applying adjustments, particularly to the area that you've picked. Adjustments to exposure, contrast, color, and maybe even other characteristics may fall under this category, depending on the goals of your artistic endeavor.

- Once you have applied your revisions, you should evaluate the changes to make sure they are what you expected. If any changes are required, you can go back and make them using the "**Select**" tool or any of the other tools that are accessible in the "**Develop**" module.

- When you have finished making revisions and are happy with them, you must remember to save your changes. Lightroom Classic will normally save your adjustments to the library automatically, but you also have the option to export the picture once it has been changed.

How to use the select background feature

Follow the steps below to use the select background feature:

- After launching Adobe Lightroom Classic, import the photo that you want to edit into the app.

- When the picture has been successfully imported, go to the "**Develop**" module by selecting the "**Develop**" tab located in the upper right-hand corner of the screen.

- The toolbar should be located on the right-hand side of the screen.

- Choose either the Adjustment Brush (keyboard shortcut: 'K') or the Graduated Filter (keyboard shortcut: 'M'. The option that you go with is determined by whether you want the impact to be applied worldwide or gradually throughout a particular region.

- If you are using the Adjustment Brush, make sure that the parameters for Size, Feather, Flow, and Density are adjusted to your liking. These variables determine the width and pressure of the brush strokes that are produced.

- In the settings panel for the Adjustment Brush or the Graduated Filter, go down to see the options for adjusting the exposure, contrast, and saturation, among other things. Make the necessary adjustments here to get the look you want for the backdrop.

- If you are going to use the Adjustment Brush, begin painting over the parts of the image that you want to change. If you are using the Graduated Filter, you can click and drag inside the image to progressively apply the filter to a certain portion of the picture.

- After making the necessary modifications, you should probably go back and tweak your pick. If you are using the Adjustment Brush, you can use the **Erase brush** to erase the effect from certain sections of the image, or you can use it to change the location and strength of the Graduated Filter.

- To fine-tune the appearance of the backdrop more generally, make use of other adjustment tools such as the Tone Curve, HSL/Color, or Effects panels.

- To compare the unaltered and changed versions of the document, use the shortcut key **'Y'** to toggle the **'Before and After'** view. *(NB: This makes it easier for you to ensure that you are attaining the backdrop effect that you want).*

- When you are happy with the way the changes have turned out, go to the **"File"** menu and choose "**Export**" to save the modified picture.

CHAPTER FOUR

Navigating the Library Module

How to import and organize photos

Importing Photos:

- First of all, launch **Adobe Lightroom Classic 2024**.

- Either connect your camera to your computer or insert the memory card that contains the pictures you want to import onto your computer.

- Find the "**Import**" button on the left-hand panel of the Library module. *(NB: This button is located on the left-hand panel).*

- Within the Import window, go to the "**Source**" panel located on the left side of the window.

- Determine the source of the image, which might be a linked camera or a certain folder on your computer.

- When you pick a source, Lightroom will show thumbnails of the photos included inside that source.

- Look through the photos and choose the ones you want to import from the list.

- Customize the options for working with files, such as copying or relocating files, and decide whether or not to create a second duplicate and save it in a different spot.

- You have the option to apply to develop settings while the image is being imported.

These options include adding metadata, and keywords or develop presets.

- Select a location to save your imported photos in the "**Destination**" panel located on the right side of the screen.

- You can arrange based on the date, the place, or into a particular folder structure.

- To maintain the order of the files, you have the option to rename them based on a template that you have created yourself.

- If you have presets, you can use them to instantly improve your images by applying them throughout the import process.

- After you have finished configuring the import settings, click the "**Import**" button to put the chosen photographs into the Lightroom catalog that you have created.

Organizing Photos:

- Navigate to the Library module to arrange and manage the photos you've imported.

- Locate the "**Folders**" area on the panel on the left side of the screen. This shows the structure of your folders depending on the import options you've chosen.

- If you want to arrange images that are linked together, you might think about establishing collections. Collections are essentially digital folders that have no bearing on the actual storage locations of your data.

- To make finding and organizing your photos easier, add relevant keywords and metadata to each one.

- You can mark your favorite images with flags and give them scores, as well as indicate which ones need more attention.

- Make use of the filter bar to whittle down your options depending on various criteria such as flags, ratings, keywords, and so on.

- Navigate to the Develop module if you want to make more in-depth changes to your images, and then use the many tools at your disposal to improve them.

- After you have arranged and modified your photos, you will be able to export them so that they may be shared with other people.

How to rate and flag images

The process of organizing and maintaining your picture collection in Adobe Lightroom Classic requires taking critical actions such as rating and flagging photographs.

Here are the steps:

Import your Photos:

It is necessary to import the photos into Adobe Lightroom Classic before you can grade and flag them.

- Launch Adobe Lightroom Classic 2024.

- Simply navigate your way to the top-right-hand area of the user interface and choose the "**Library**" module.

- To access the "**Import**" dialog, click the "**Import**" button located in the bottom left corner of the screen.

Rate your Images:

After your pictures have been imported, you will be able to begin ranking them according to their significance, quality, or any other criterion you want.

Grid View:

- Navigate to the "**Library**" section of the module.

- Pressing the "**G**" key will take you to the "**Grid View**" option.

- Choose the pictures you want to rate before continuing.

Use the Quick Develop Panel:

- The "**Quick Develop**" panel can be found on the right-hand side of the screen.

- Navigate to the "**Set Flag**" and "**Set Rating**" options on the menu.

- Select the appropriate rating (from 1 to 5 stars) or flag (Flagged, Unflagged, Rejected) for each of the photos that have been chosen.

Filter and Sort Images:

Once you've given each of your photos a rating, you'll have the ability to quickly filter and arrange them depending on these criteria.

Filter Bar:

- The "**Filter Bar**" is found in the upper-right corner of the Grid module.

- To filter photos according to flags, ratings, or other criteria, use the available dropdown menus.

Library Filter:

- Use the "**Library Filter**" option located on the top bar of the Library module.

- Select certain groups of photos to show by selecting criteria such as flags, ratings, and other options.

Flagging Images for Quick Selection:

During the culling process, marking photographs with flags makes it easier to immediately identify and organize the photos that need to be removed.

Flagging Shortcuts:

- To mark an item as Pick, use the "**P**" key.

- To remove the flag, use the "**U**" key.

- To decline, use the "**X**" button.

How to use filters and smart collections

Using Filters:

- Launch Adobe Lightroom Classic and go to the catalog where all of your photos are stored.

- Navigate to the "**Library**" tab at the very top of the screen and click there.

- In the Library module, the Filter Bar for the Library may be found at the very top of the grid view.

- To filter the results, click the name of the attribute (Text, Attribute, Metadata, etc.) that you wish to use.

- You can, for instance, filter the results using keywords, flags, ratings, or other types of information.

- To fine-tune the filter, choose certain numbers, ranges, or keywords to search for.

- This assists you in isolating the photos that you want to use in your project.

- Once you have applied your filters, the grid view will only show you photographs that correspond to the criteria that you have chosen to display.

Working with Smart Collections

- In the Library module, go to the left side of the interface and choose the Collections panel.

- To create a new smart collection, right-click, and choose "**Create Smart Collection**."

- When the dialog box displays, you will be able to set the criteria for your Smart Collection.

- This may contain search terms, ratings, file kinds, and other information as well.

- Give your Smart Collection a name that means a lot to you so that you can quickly determine its function.

- Look over the selection criteria and make sure they line up with what you had in mind.

- Confirm the creation of the Smart Collection by clicking either the **"Create"** or **"Save"** button.

- Smart Collections will automatically update themselves depending on the criteria that you choose.

- Any new photos that are uploaded and satisfy the requirements will have them included immediately.

- To make changes to a Smart Collection, right-click on the collection in question, and choose **"Edit Smart Collection."**

- Make the necessary changes to the criteria, and then click **"Save."**

- If you find that you no longer need a Smart Collection, right-click on it, and then choose "**Delete**."

How to set up different view modes on Lightroom Classic

Using a variety of modules and tools is required in Adobe Lightroom Classic to configure the different view modes.

Here are the steps:

- Begin by opening the Adobe Lightroom Classic app that is installed on your computer.

- Make sure that you have imported and arranged all of your photos in the Library module before you begin configuring the display modes.

- In the top-right corner of the user interface, choose the **Library module** and click on it.

- You should categorize and label your photos by using different keywords, flags, and star ratings.

- To see many photos all at once, go to the Grid view inside the Library module.

- Use the slider located at the bottom of the screen to change the size of the thumbnails.

- To study a single picture in more detail, enter loupe view by double-clicking on that image or using the "**E**" key on your keyboard.

- In the Library module, choose at least two and no more than three photographs.

- To enter the Compare view, use the "**C**" key on your keyboard. You may zoom in and move around to examine chosen photos from different angles and perspectives.

- Select numerous photos from the available options in the Library module.

- To enter Survey view, use the "**N**" key on your keyboard. In this mode, you may see chosen photographs side by side and make comparisons.

- To make alterations to individual photos, you will need to go to the Develop module.

- To alter the exposure, contrast, color balance, and other settings, use the panels located on the right.

- You can organize your images into collections based on topics, projects, or any other criterion by using Collections.

- The left panel of the Library module is where you'll find the Collections section.

- In the Develop module, you can create presets for often-used modifications and store them for later use.

- When you are finished organizing and editing your images, you can use the Export tool to store them or share them with others.

- Make sure you regularly back up your Lightroom library to avoid losing any of your data.

- If you are working on numerous projects at once, you should manage catalogs to keep them organized.

How to organize your photos with metadata and keywords

Importing Photos:

- Launch Adobe Lightroom Classic 2024 on your PC.

- If your photos are stored on a memory card or camera, connect it to your computer and use the "**Import**" window in Lightroom Classic to transfer the images to your library. If your photos are stored on a memory card, connect your camera to your computer.

- In the Import dialog, you can pick your import options, including where to store your images and how to arrange them. *(NB: You can create folders according to the date, location, or based on your criteria).*

- Find the "**Apply During Import**" area in the right panel of the Import dialog. This will allow you to apply metadata during the import process. You can also apply metadata presets that include information on copyright, keywords, and other specifics in this section.

- To import the photos into your Lightroom library, click the "**Import**" option after you have finished configuring your settings and before you do anything else.

Adding Metadata

- **Library Module**: In Lightroom Classic, choose the Library module to access its features.

- **Grid View**: To see a larger number of photos at once, you can switch to the Grid view.

- **Choose Photos**: Choose the photos to which you would want to add information.

- **Metadata Panel**: The Metadata panel can be found on the right-hand side of the screen. You have the option of including a variety of facts, such as information on copyright, captions, and keywords, in this section.

- **Add Keywords**: In the box labeled "**Keywording**," put pertinent keywords while separating them with commas. For instance, if you have photos that you took while on a trip to the beach, you may include keywords such as **"beach," "vacation," "sunset,"** and so on.

- **Apply Presets to Metadata:** If you have certain metadata presets stored elsewhere, you may apply them here. **(NB: This helps provide information that is consistent across many photos in a group).**

Using Keywords

- **Organize Keywords**: You can organize your keywords by creating hierarchies in the Keyword List panel, which is located on the right side of the screen. For instance, under "**Travel**," you can have sub-keywords like "**Europe**," "**Asia**," etc.

- **Apply Keywords in Bulk**: To apply keywords to many photos at once, choose the photos you want to edit and then drag them onto the applicable keywords in the Keyword List. You can now apply keywords in bulk thanks to this feature.

- **Filter by Keywords:** You can filter photographs based on keywords by using the Filter Bar that is located above the Grid view. This makes it simple to locate certain photographs at a later time.

Advanced Organization

- **Collections**: Regardless of where your images are stored on your hard drive, you may create collections to organize similar pictures into themed sets.

- **Labels, Stars, and Flags**: To further organize and prioritize your photos, you can make use of flags, star ratings, and color-coded labels.

- **Face Recognition:** Lightroom Classic's features include the ability to recognize faces. Make use of this tool to categorize and arrange images following the people in them.

Backing up your Catalog

- **Regular Backups**: To avoid any loss of data, make sure that you back up your Lightroom library regularly. Use cloud services or external drives to increase the level of security.

- **Smart Previews:** If you're concerned about storage space, you may want to think about generating Smart Previews for your photos. These are more manageable, compact versions of the original files that enable you to continue working on your photographs even when the original files are disconnected.

How to do selective editing

Follow the steps below to apply selective editing:

- First, launch Adobe Lightroom Classic, and then import the photographs that need editing.

- To make the administration of your photo library simpler, organize your pictures into collections or folders.

- To access the "**Develop**" module, either hit the "**D**" key on your keyboard or click the "**Develop**" module situated in the upper right.

- To make global changes to your picture, use the basic sliders in the panel on the right-hand side of the screen. This includes things like exposure, contrast, highlights, and shadows, among other things.

- To use the "**Graduated** Filter" tool, go to the tool's location right above the Basic panel and click on it.

- To create a gradient effect on your picture, click and drag with your mouse.

- Modify the settings such as exposure, temperature, or saturation to adjust the gradient's coverage of a specific section of the image selectively.

- The Radial Filter, which is quite similar to the Graduated Filter, provides you with the ability to make modifications in a circular pattern.

- To alter a specific area, choose the "**Radial Filter**" tool from the drop-down menu, and then draw an ellipse around that region.

- Make necessary adjustments to the settings.

- To adjust the brush's settings, use the "**Adjustment Brush**" tool, which can be found next to the Radial Filter.

- Use the brush tool to go over the precise region that has to be edited.

- Change the settings for things like exposure, contrast, and sharpness.

- To carefully edit certain colors in your photograph, use the HSL/Color panel in Adobe Photoshop.

- For instance, the saturation of the blue sky may be increased without affecting the other colors in the image.

- If you want to make exact alterations to the tone, use the Tone Curve panel.

- You can construct points on the curve to make specific adjustments to the shadows, highlights, or mid-tones.

- Experiment with different correction presets and apply them to your shot to improve certain parts of it.

- Create your custom presets to get a uniform appearance across a variety of photos.

- To make local alterations, such as getting rid of blemishes or other unsightly things, use the tool called "**Spot Removal.**"

- Crop your photo such that the attention is drawn to certain aspects of it.

- To switch between the unaltered and changed versions, use the backslash key ("") on your keyboard.

- Evaluate the effects of your modifications and make any required adjustments.

- Once you are pleased with the changes you made, go to the "**Library**" module.

- First, choose the photos you want to export, then make any necessary adjustments to the export parameters, and last, export your newly altered images.

CHAPTER FIVE

How to adjust white balance and

color temperature

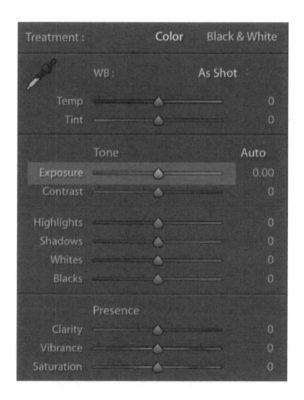

- To edit a picture, load it into Adobe Lightroom Classic.

- In the upper right corner of the screen, click the "**Develop**" module.

- Locate the "**Basic**" panel in the right panel. At the top of this panel are the White Balance controls.

- White Balance presets in Lightroom include Auto, Daylight, Cloudy, Shade, Tungsten, Fluorescent, and Flash. To see how these settings impact your picture, click on them. This is a fast technique to get a solid foundation.

- The temperature and tint sliders can be manually adjusted if the presets don't provide the desired outcome.

➢ **Temperature Slider:** The picture becomes colder (more blue) when the slider is moved to the left; it becomes warmer (more yellow) when it is moved to the right.

➢ **Tint Slider:** Exacting a leftward adjustment adds more green; an upward adjustment adds more magenta.

- Select the "**WB**" tool by clicking on it (it's the one with the temperature and tint sliders on the left). With the use of this tool, you can click anywhere in your shot that is neutral, and Lightroom will automatically alter the white balance depending on that choice.

- Adjust the various color channels more if necessary. To access the sliders for varying the strength of individual colors, click on the "**Color**" panel.

- Use the "**Y**" key to access the before/after mode or the backslash key "" to compare your adjustments with the original picture.

- After making the necessary corrections, you can return to the Library module or click "**Done**" in the Develop module to preserve your modifications.

- Go to the Library module, choose the altered picture, and then click **Export** if you want to share or use it elsewhere other than Lightroom.

How to use the histogram

One of the most useful tools in Adobe Lightroom Classic is the histogram, which shows you the tonal distribution of your image. It shows how highlights, midtones, and shadows are shared.

Follow the steps below to use the histogram in Adobe Lightroom Classic:

- To edit a photo, import it into Adobe Lightroom Classic.

- Select the "**Develop**" tab located in the upper-right area to access the Develop module.

- Usually found under the basic adjustment panels at the top of the Develop module, is the histogram.

- The tonal range is represented by the horizontal axis, which runs from black on the left to white on the right.

- The quantity of pixels at each tonal level is shown on the vertical axis.

- To change your image's overall brightness, use the **Exposure slider** in the Basic panel.

- Keep an eye on the histogram to make sure it doesn't clip at the extremes, touching the edges, since this suggests that there is a loss of clarity in the highlights or shadows.

- To change the contrast between the bright and dark portions of your picture, move the Contrast slider up or down in the Basic panel.

- To modify certain tonal ranges, use the sliders in the Basic panel. For instance, shift the Highlights slider to the left to restore highlight detail.

- Red, Green, and Blue are the three channels that often make up a histogram. If you move your cursor over the histogram, you can view specific channel data.

- More sophisticated tonal changes are possible using the Tone Curve panel. The curve may have points added to it to modify certain tonal ranges.

- To see places where detail has been lost, enable the clipping warnings (triangle icons at the upper corners of the histogram). The triangles on the left and right represent shadows and highlights, respectively.

- Color casts can be identified using the histogram. You may need to change the color balance if one color channel is more prominent than the others.

- Once you've made any necessary revisions, remember to save them.

- By choosing "**Export**" from the File menu, you can export the altered picture in many different formats.

- Feel free to try out various tweaks and see how the histogram changes as a result.

- Using the History panel on the left, you can reverse changes if necessary.

How to adjust exposure, contrast, and saturation

Changing the Exposure:

- To begin editing, open Adobe Lightroom Classic and import the picture.

- Click the "**Develop**" tab at the top of the screen to open the "**Develop**" module.

- The "**Basic**" panel is located in the panel on the right. *(NB: This is the area where exposure, contrast, and saturation are adjusted).*

- Locate the "**Exposure**" slider and drag it to the left to reduce exposure or to the right to enhance it. Get a real-time preview of the changes.

Changing the Contrast:

- Find the "**Contrast**" slider in the "**Basic**" panel.

- To enhance or reduce contrast, move the "**Contrast**" slider to the right or left. This contrasts the bright and dark portions of your image more pronounced.

Changing the Saturation:

- Once again, locate the "**Saturation**" slider in the "**Basic**" panel.

- Slide the "**Saturation**" slider to the left to desaturate the picture, or to the right to intensify the colors. Take care not to go overboard since photos that are too saturated might seem artificial.

Fine-Tuning:

- **Use the Tone Curve:** The Tone Curve may be used for more complex modifications. You can manually modify the tone curve to have exact control over the highlights, shadows, and midtones by selecting the "**Tone Curve**" option.

- **Modify HSL/Color Panel:** Open the "**HSL/Color**" panel to make modifications that are unique to the color. *(NB: This is where you adjust the brightness, hue, and saturation of particular colors).*

- **Use Graduated Filters and Adjustment Brushes:** These tools can be used to make alterations that are localized. With the help of these tools, you can make modifications to certain areas of your picture alone.

- **Before-and-After View**: Press the "" key to see a side-by-side comparison of your adjustments and the original, or use the "**Y**" key to compare them.

- **Export Your picture**: To save your altered picture, click the "**File**" menu and choose "**Export**" when you're happy with your changes.

How to create a black-and-white matte look

Tonality, contrast, and matte effect adjustments are combined in Adobe Lightroom Classic 2024 to create a black-and-white matte style for your images.

Here are the steps:

- To begin editing, load the picture into Adobe Lightroom Classic.

- Select **Develop** from the menu.

- Adjust the Tint and Temperature in the Basic section to your liking. For a matte effect, colder temperatures usually work best.

- To get a well-balanced tonal range, make adjustments to the Exposure, Contrast, Highlights, Shadows, Whites, and Blacks. To achieve the ideal balance for your image, try different things.

- Move down to the HSL/Color/B&W panel.

- To convert your picture to black and white, choose the "**B&W**" option.

- Adjust the brightness of each color using the sliders in the Black & White Mix section of the same panel. This lets you adjust the black-

and-white image's brightness for individual components.

- Select the Presence panel and modify the Dehaze and Clarity sliders. To preserve a softer, matte look, use these modifications sparingly.

- Locate and choose the **Tone Curve panel**.

- Add points to the curve, raise the highlights a little, and reduce the shadows to create a soft "S" shape. This creates a matte effect and improves contrast.

- Give the highlights and shadows in the Split Toning panel a splash of color. To produce a slight color difference, use a warmer tone for highlights and a cooler tone for shadows.

- Proceed to the Effects panel.

- To create a faint vignette, move the Amount slider up under the Post-Crop Vignetting section. To perfect the vignette effect, play around with the Midpoint and Roundness values.

- Navigate to the Detail panel.

- To give your picture a texture reminiscent of a movie, move the Amount slider up beneath the Grain area. To manipulate how the grain looks, play with the Size and Roughness settings.

- Adjust any more parameters as necessary. Try adjusting the sliders until you get the desired matte black-and-white effect.

- After making the necessary adjustments, click the "**File**" menu and choose "**Export**" to save your picture.

How to use dodge and burn for black-and-white photos

Import and Basic Adjustments

- Upon launching Adobe Lightroom Classic, import your black-and-white photo.

- Make the first necessary changes in the Develop module. To achieve a solid starting point, adjust the exposure, contrast, highlights, and shadows.

- Click "**Develop**" in the upper right corner to get to the Develop module.

- To use the Adjustment Brush tool, locate it on the right panel and hit the letter **'K'** on your keyboard.

Dodge (Brighten) with Adjustment Brush

- Adjust the Dodge brush settings. Boost exposure to brighter places.

- You can adjust the effect by optionally adjusting other variables, such as Highlights and Whites.

- Gently scrub the parts you want to make brighter. Usually, highlights are used for this, highlighting features in brighter places.

- To manage the severity of the dodge effect, lower the brush opacity if the effect is too strong.

Use an Adjustment Brush to Burn (Darken)

- Select **Burn** for the brush settings. Reduce Your Exposure to Dim Areas.

- You can optionally fine-tune the effect by adjusting the Shadows and Blacks.

- Use a brush to enhance shadows and add depth to sections of your picture that you want to deepen.

- To modify the intensity of the burn effect, adjust the brush opacity like Dodge.

Graduated Filters for Dodge and Burn

- Press **'M'** to activate the Graduated Filter tool and use it to gradually brighten the image. Move the filter in the direction of the darker area from the brighter area.

- For a progressively darker look, use the Graduated Filter in the same manner. Drag the dark area in the direction of the brighter area.

Fine-Tune with Radial Filters

Dodge and Burn Dial Filter:

- Use radial filters (**'Shift+M'**) to adjust the brightness or darkness of certain areas of your picture. Modify the configuration as necessary.

Refine and Review:

- To examine and fine-tune your changes, zoom in. Make sure that the burn and dodge effects accentuate details without resulting in information loss or overexposure.

- You can switch between the original and modified versions by using the **backslash key** ("). This enables you to observe how your dodge and burn modifications are affecting things.

- Adjust the overall sharpness, contrast, and tone as necessary.

- After you're happy, export your picture to the size and format you choose.

CHAPTER SIX

Exploring the Develop Module

How to understand basic editing tools

- Launch Lightroom Classic and choose the "**Import**" option from the menu that appears.

- Select the photos that you want to modify and then choose the folder that they will be saved to.

- If it is essential, you should apply metadata, and keywords, and develop settings as the import is happening.

- Become familiar with the Library module so that you can organize and manage your photographs more effectively.

- To mark and organize your photographs, you may make use of flags, stars, and color labels.

- To begin the real editing process, go to the Develop module. The major editing tools can be found in the panel on the right.

Basic Panel:

White Balance:

- Change the color temperature to either warm or chill the overall appearance of your photo.
- The ratio of green to magenta is determined by the tint.

Exposure:

- Adjust the level of brightness across the whole picture.

Contrast:

- Make the contrast between the bright and dark parts more or less pronounced.

Highlights, the shadows, the whites, blacks:

- For more control, make precise adjustments to certain tonal ranges.

Tone Curve:

- To make exact modifications, modify the tonal range using the graph editor.

- Make the necessary adjustments to the curve for the highlights, lights, and darks.

HSL/Color Panel:

Hue, Saturation, and Luminance: Luminance:

- Make exact adjustments to the colors in your photo.

Detail Panel:

- This provides access to sharpening as well as noise-reduction tools.

- To sharpen the image, adjust the amount, the radius, the detail, and the masking.

Lens Corrections:

- Make the necessary adjustments to correct the distortion, chromatic aberration, and vignetting.

- To remove chromatic aberration and enable profile corrections, enable the "**Remove**

Chromatic Aberration" and "**Enable Profile Corrections**" settings.

Effects Panel:

Post-Crop Vignetting:

- Make adjustments to the vignette so that the focus is brought to the center.

Grain:

- To give your shot a retro look, try adding grain to it as a film would.

How to adjust exposure, color, and tone

Adjusting Exposure:

- Launch Adobe Lightroom Classic on your PC.

- Bring the photos you want to edit into your catalog by doing the appropriate imports.

- To access the "**Develop**" module, go to the upper right corner of the screen and choose the "**Develop**" tab.

- The "**Basic**" panel is found in the panel on the right-hand side. Controls controlling the amount of exposure are included in this section.

- Move the slider labeled "**Exposure**" up or down to change the overall level of brightness in your photo.

- If you want to do more extensive exposure changes, use the Tone Curve panel.

- To modify the curve for the highlights, shadows, and midtones, go to the Tone Curve tab and click on it.

Adjusting Color:

- The "**White Balance**" area is found in the "**Basic**" tab of the editing interface.

- Adjust the temperature and tint by dragging the appropriate sliders or by using the eyedropper tool to remove any color cast.

- Go to the "**HSL/Color**" panel in the panel menu.

- To modify the hue, saturation, and luminosity of particular colors, use the sliders located in the **"Hue," "Saturation,"** and "**Luminance**" tabs.

- To add color tones to the highlights and shadows, go to the "**Split Toning**" tab on your editing toolbar.

Adjusting Tone:

- To improve the contrast in your image as a whole, use the "**Contrast**" slider located in the "**Basic**" panel.

- To increase the contrast between the midtones, use the "**Clarity**" slider.

- Drag the "**Dehaze**" slider to the left or right to adjust the amount of haze in the image.

- The Tone Curve panel is an effective tool for fine-tuning the instrument's tones. Make any necessary adjustments to the curve to affect the highlights, shadows, and midtones.

- Make alterations to certain parts of your photograph by making use of these tools, which allow you to target specific locations.

- To make fine-grained modifications, use the Adjustment Brush tool and paint changes onto the areas that need them.

Keep in mind that you should always preview your modifications by contrasting the version that has been altered with the original. You can do this by using the backslash key ("") or by using the "**Y**" key to toggle the "**Before/After**" view. Both of these keys are located in the top-right corner of your keyboard. When you are finished making alterations to your picture and are happy with the results, you can export it to keep the changes.

How to crop and straighten photos

Here are the steps:

- First of all, open Adobe Lightroom Classic 2024.

- To begin editing your images, first import them into the library of your Lightroom Classic software. You can do this by going to the "**Import**" option on the toolbar and then choosing the directory on your computer where your pictures are stored.

- After you have imported your photos, go to the "**Develop**" module. To do this, choose the "**Develop**" tab located in the upper-right-hand corner of the screen and click on it.

- In the filmstrip located at the bottom of the page, choose the photo that you want to crop and then straighten.

- To use the "**Crop Overlay**" tool, locate it in the right panel, and then click on it. By doing this, the crop and straighten choices will become active.

- To make changes to the crop, drag the corners of the crop box to the desired position. You can also reposition the crop by moving the whole box in the editor. You can also choose one of the options located in the toolbar at the very top of the screen to preserve a certain aspect ratio.

- To correct crookedness in your photograph, drag the cursor outside the area that will be cropped until you see it transform into an arrow with two points. You can straighten lines in your picture by using the mouse to click and drag along the line you want to straighten. To rectify the tilt of the image, Lightroom will make the necessary adjustments automatically.

- Additional modifications can be made by dragging the sliders located in the "**Angle**" and "**Aspect**" parts of the right panel. Both the "**Angle**" slider, which enables more exact rotation, and the "**Aspect**" slider, which enables changes to the aspect ratio, are located on the same panel.

- To make the crop and straightening modifications, you can either click the "**Done**" button or press the "**Enter**" key on your keyboard.

- When you are happy with the changes that have been made, you can export the picture that has been modified by going to the "**File**" menu and choosing "**Export.**" *(NB: After that, you can choose the export settings and the folder where the photo will be saved).*

How to use the retouch and spot removal tool

Retouch Tool:

The Retouch tool in Adobe Lightroom Classic is used to remove major flaws or undesired features from the photographs you've taken.

- After launching Adobe Lightroom Classic, import the image that has to be edited into the program.

- To access the "**Develop**" module, click on the "**Develop**" tab located in the top right corner of the screen. *(NB: This will take you to the "Develop" module).*

- Navigate to the toolbar on the right-hand side of the panel, and either click on the "**Spot Removal**" tool or hit the "**Q**" key on your keyboard to activate it.

- You CAN change the size of the brush by using the [and] keys on your keyboard or by dragging the slider shown in the toolbar. This is dependent on the magnitude of the flaw that you wish to retouch.

- To retouch a specific region, you must first click on that area. Lightroom will choose an area from the immediate surroundings to take a sample from automatically.

- If the automated selection does not provide an optimal result, you can manually alter the source point by dragging it to a more appropriate location.

- When you are pleased with the results of the retouching, either click the **"Done"** button located in the toolbar or hit the **"Enter"** key on your keyboard.

Spot Removal Tool:

The Spot Removal tool is useful for eradicating tiny flaws, such as dust spots or blemishes, off the surface of an object.

- In the Develop module, either hit the **'Q'** key on your keyboard or pick the **"Spot Removal"** tool.

- Determine the size of the place that you wish to remove, and then use either the [and] keys on your keyboard or the slider in the toolbar to change the size of the brush.

- To correct an imperfection, you must first select it by clicking on it. Lightroom will choose an area from the immediate vicinity to use as a substitute automatically.

- If necessary, manually adjust the source point by dragging it to a better location to match the target.

- When you are finished making adjustments, either click the "**Done**" button located in the toolbar or hit the "**Enter**" button to save your modifications.

- Perform the procedure once again for any defect or location that may be found in the picture.

- To remove spots with more accuracy, zoom in on the picture using either the zoom tool or the **'Z'** key on your keyboard.

- If you make a mistake, you can reverse the modifications by hitting the **'Ctrl + Z'** key combination (on Windows) or the 'Cmd + Z' key combination (on Mac). Alternatively, you may undo modifications by using the shortcut 'Ctrl + Y' (on Windows) or 'Cmd + Y' (on Mac).

How to use presets and profiles

Using Presets:

- Launch Adobe Lightroom Classic 2024.

- To begin editing your images, first import them into the library of your Lightroom Classic software.

- Once your photos have been imported, go to the "**Develop**" module by either using the "**D**" key on your keyboard or clicking on the "**Develop**" tab located in the top-right corner of the screen.

- You can locate the Presets panel in the Develop module by looking to the left side of the screen. To make the panel visible, expand it by clicking on the tiny triangle in the upper right corner.

- Lightroom Classic comes with a selection of presets that are considered to be the default, but you also have the option to import your own presets. Simply clicking on the preset you want to use is all that is required to apply it. Your picture will now reflect the adjustments that have been made.

- After applying a preset, you can further personalize your photograph by modifying the options in the panels on the right-hand side of the screen. A few examples of these include exposure, contrast, highlights, and shadows, among others.

- Create your own presets if you have made certain modifications that you would want to preserve for future usage in the form of a preset. To create a new preset, go to the Presets panel, click the "+" symbol, give your preset a name, and then choose the parameters you wish to include.

Using Profiles:

- Similar to how you would access the presets in Lightroom Classic, go to the "**Develop**" module.

- The Profile Browser is found on the right-hand side of the screen, just below the Basic panel. If it is not already obvious, choose the "**Profile**" tab.

- Many different default profiles are included with the Lightroom Classic download. Simply selecting the desired persona and clicking the "**Apply**" button will cause the modifications to be made to your profile picture.

- Some profiles could contain a slider labeled "**intensity**" that gives you the ability to adjust the level of the profile's effect. Adjusting the effect may be done using the slider located here.

- Lightroom Classic also allows you to create your unique profiles. To do this, go to the Profile Browser, choose the "+" button, and then pick the settings that you want to include in your profile from the drop-down menu that appears.

How to make basic adjustments to your photos

The steps:

- To begin, open Adobe Lightroom Classic 2024.

- In the Library module, choose the "**Import**" button to begin the import process.

- After locating the folder that has your images, choose the edited photos.

- Select the appropriate options for your import, then click "**Import**."

- At the very top of the screen, choose the "**Develop**" module and click on it.

Basic Adjustments

White Balance:

- Make the necessary adjustments to the white balance to get the color temperature precisely right.

- To get the desired effect, adjust the White Balance using either the tool or the sliders.

Exposure:

- Adjust the exposure settings to regulate the photo's level of overall brightness.

- Make the necessary adjustments to the Exposure slider.

Contrast:

- Adjust the contrast in your shot by either increasing it or decreasing it to add or remove drama.

- To make this modification, move the Contrast slider up or down.

Highlights and Shadows:

- Bring back features that were lost in places that were either overexposed (the highlights) or underexposed (the shadows).

- Move the sliders for the Highlights and Shadows effects.

Whites and Blacks:

- To get a wider variety of tonalities, you should adjust the white and black points.

- To see clipping, you must first press and hold the Alt key (or the Option key on a Mac) while moving the Whites or Blacks slider.

Saturation and Vibrance:

- Raise or lower the saturation level of the colors.

- To adjust the overall color intensity, use the Saturation slider, and to safeguard skin tones, use the Vibrance slider.

Detail Adjustments

Sharpening:

- Make your picture sharper by enhancing its contrast.

- Move the sliders for the Amount, Radius, and Detail to the desired values.

Noise Reduction:

- Reduce the amount of noise in your image, particularly in low-light settings.

- Move the Luminance and Color sliders around in the Detail panel to get the desired effect.

Lens Corrections

Profile Corrections:

- Adjust the chromatic aberrations and distortions caused by the lens.

- In the Lens Corrections panel, choose the "**Enable Profile Corrections**" option and click the "**Enable**" button.

- If necessary, make manual adjustments to the amount of distortion, vignetting, and chromatic aberration.

How to use a texture slider

The Texture slider in Adobe Lightroom Classic allows you to increase or decrease the amount of fine detail in the photos you take. It is very helpful for providing a little sharpening effect or for smoothing out certain sections of the image. The following is an in-depth tutorial on how to make use of the Texture slider:

Here are the steps:

- Open **Adobe Lightroom Classic** and then import the image that needs to be edited. You may begin making edits to your picture as soon as it is loaded into either the Library or Develop module.

- To begin, go to the top-right corner of the screen and choose the "**Develop**" module. All of the editing tools, such as the Texture slider, are located in this section of the editor.

- Locate the "**Basic**" panel on the right-hand side of the window. The Texture slider is often positioned just below the Clarity slider in most instances. If you are unable to locate it, search for the "**Presence**" area. It is part of the tools that improve the overall sharpness and clarity of the picture.

- By moving the Texture slider to the right, you can enhance the texture of the image, which will highlight the finer elements. When you drag it to the left, you can reduce the texture, which will result in a smoother overall appearance.

- Keep an eye on the changes occurring in your picture as you move the Texture slider. Increase the magnification to notice how the adjustment impacts the various areas of the picture, particularly the areas that contain complex features.

- Use the Masking slider to choose exactly where the texture alteration is applied to the image. While holding down the **Alt or Option key**, move the slider to expose the regions that will be impacted (areas that are white) and the areas that will be protected (black areas). This allows you to tailor the texture modification to certain parts of the photo.

- The overall quality of the picture may be improved in several ways, one of which is by adding texture. You can obtain the style you want for your picture by adjusting some of the other settings, such as Clarity, Sharpening, and Noise Reduction.

- You can examine the results of your changes by using the backslash key () to switch between the unaltered and altered versions of the photograph you are viewing.

- When you've finished making edits and are happy with the results, you may save the picture that you've modified. You can save it in the format and location of your choosing by selecting "**Export**" from the "**File**" menu.

CHAPTER SEVEN

How to create virtual copies

The ability to create virtual copies of a picture in Adobe Lightroom Classic is a valuable tool that enables you to experiment with various alterations or versions of the same image without having those changes made to the original file.

Here's how to create virtual copies in Lightroom Classic:

- Launch Adobe Lightroom Classic 2024.

- It will be necessary for you to import your photos into your Lightroom library if they are not already there. Select the photos you want to use for your project after clicking the "**Import**" button located in the Library module.

- To access the Library module, choose the "**Library**" tab located in the panel's top-left corner and click on it.

- Find the image that you want to use as a template for the virtual copy at the bottom of the screen, either in the Filmstrip view or the Grid view.

Create a Virtual Copy

There are a few different techniques to generate a virtual clone, including the following:

Right-Click Method:

- ➤ Proceed to right-click on the image.
- ➤ From the option that appears, pick "**Create Virtual Copy**."

- When you have completed the steps necessary to pick the right approach, you will see that a new thumbnail has been added next to the first picture. *(NB: **The digital copy is now complete and ready to be edited independently**).*

- You are now able to make any changes or modifications to the virtual copy without having those changes reflected in the original picture or any other virtual copies that you may generate in the future.

- Repeat the procedure by choosing the first virtual copy or any other copy that already exists, and then make a new copy to generate other virtual copies to conduct further experiments.

- To examine the various changes, you should go back and forth between the original and the virtual copy. You can examine the changes side by side by using the "**Before and After**" view options in the editing tool.

- After you have finished making modifications and are pleased with them, you have the option to export the virtual copies or share them as necessary.

How to create snapshots

The steps:

- Launch **Adobe Lightroom Classic 2024**.

- Import the photos that you want to edit into the Lightroom catalog that you are using. You can do this by choosing the pictures you want to import from their storage location after clicking the "**Import**" button.

- Access the Develop module by selecting the "**Develop**" tab which is located in the upper-right-hand corner of the screen.

- The Develop module provides you with a wide variety of tools and panels that you may use to make the necessary adjustments to your shot. To get the desired appearance, play about with the settings for things like exposure, contrast, and white balance, among others.

- Find the panel labeled "**Snapshot**" on the left side of the Develop module. You may make it visible by either typing the "S" key on your keyboard or clicking the little triangle that is located next to the "**Snapshots**" label if it is not already visible.

- To add snapshot, choose the "**Snapshot**" panel and then select the "+" icon. By performing this operation, a new snapshot will be created, which will save your picture in its present condition together with any adjustments that have been done.

- When you click the + button, a dialogue window will open, asking you what name you would want to give your picture. Enter a name that is illustrative and will assist you in identifying the modifications or changes that were done at that specific stage of the editing process.

- You can make several snapshots at various points during the editing process. This gives you the ability to evaluate the differences between several versions or to return to a previous stage in the editing process.

- Simply clicking on the name of the snapshot in the "**Snapshot**" window will allow you to move between snapshots. Your picture will get the previously stored settings when you carry out this activity.

- After you have completed your desired adjustments and chosen the appropriate snapshot, you can export your picture by heading to the "**File**" menu and selecting "**Export.**" Performing this action will store the altered version of your picture in the place that you choose.

How to sharpen and use noise reduction

Here are the steps:

- First, launch Adobe Lightroom Classic and then import the photo you wish to edit into the program.

- In the upper right-hand corner of the user interface, find the **'Develop'** module and select it with your mouse.

- Before applying sharpening, you need first make some fundamental modifications to the exposure, contrast, and other parameters.

- Zoom in until you get a view of your picture that is 1:1. This will allow you to evaluate and apply sharpening more properly.

- Navigate to the right side of the Develop module and locate the 'Detail' panel there.

Apply Sharpening:

- The level of sharpness can be adjusted by dragging the **'Amount'** slider up and down. You should begin with a setting that is cautious and progressively raise it until you get the desired level of sharpness.

- Change the value of the **'Radius'** parameter to determine the degree to which the sharpening effect is applied.

- The **'Detail'** slider helps bring out finer details without amplifying the background noise.

- The **'Masking'** slider gives you the ability to restrict sharpening to just the image's edges, protecting the smoother parts of the image from being altered.

Using the Alt Key or the Option Key:

- To see the impact of altering the sliders, you must first depress and hold the **Alt key** (or the **Option key** on a Mac). *(NB: This helps to prevent the blade from being over-sharpened).*

- To sharpen certain areas of an image, you can use the Adjustment Brush or the Graduated Filter. *(NB: This helps bring more focus to certain parts of the picture).*

The following are the steps for reducing noise in Adobe Lightroom Classic:

- In the **'Detail'** panel, scroll down until you reach the **'Noise Reduction'** area.

- Move the **'Luminance'** slider to the left to cut down on the total amount of luminance noise in your picture. Raise it until you get a result that's satisfactory in terms of noise reduction and the preservation of picture features.

- To lessen the appearance of color noise, use the **'Color'** slider. Make careful adjustments to keep the noise reduction and the preservation of color detail in harmony with one another.

- Using the **'Detail'** slider, choose the amount of detail that will be preserved in the picture after the noise reduction has been applied.

- "**Smoothness**" helps reduce the number of artifacts. Be careful not to turn it up too much, since doing so might cause the loss of fine detail in the image.

- Like that of sharpening, you may see the impact of modifying the noise reduction sliders while holding down the **Alt key** (or the Option key on Mac).

- To get a preview of the changes that the sharpening and noise reduction modifications have made, toggle the "**Before/After**" view on and off.

- When you are finished making modifications and are happy with the results, go to the 'File' menu and choose **'Export'** to save your picture.

How to use presets to speed up your workflow

The use of presets, which are settings that have already been pre-defined, enables you to give your photographs a variety of distinct appearances and styles. Your workflow for editing may be substantially sped up by making use of presets, which will enable you to make alterations to several photos in a consistent manner with just a few clicks of the mouse.

Follow the steps below to use presets to speed up your workflow:

- Open Adobe Lightroom Classic and add the photos you want to change to your library before you do anything else.

- To access the "**Develop**" module, either hit the "D" key on your keyboard or select the "**Develop**" tab located in the top-right corner of the screen.

- Locate the Presets Panel. The "**Presets**" panel can be found in the Develop module on the left-hand side of the window. You can choose to make it visible if it isn't already by clicking on the "+" symbol in the left panel and choosing "**Presets**."

- Lightroom comes preloaded with several presets, but you also have the option to download more ones or build your own. Click on the folder containing the presets you wish to investigate, and then click on a particular preset to see the impact it has on the image you have picked.

- Simply clicking on the preset's actual name will cause it to be applied. You will be able to view the adjustments made to your photograph immediately after applying the preset settings.

- Presets are a wonderful place to begin, but you may need to make some further tweaks so that they work with your particular picture. Adjust the exposure, contrast, and color balance, as well as any other parameters, by dragging the appropriate sliders in the "**Develop**" module.

- You can develop your own presets if you realize that you are often making modifications that are quite similar to one another. After making the necessary adjustments, go to the "**Presets**" panel, click the "+" button, and choose the option to "**Create Preset**." First, give your preset a name, and then choose the options that you wish to include in it.

- It is possible to apply presets to many photographs all at once, which will speed up your process. After making your selections in the Filmstrip at the bottom of the interface or in the Library module, you can then choose the preset you want to use on the photos you have chosen to alter.

- It is also possible that you'll want to tweak some variables on an individual basis before applying presets to several images. After applying the preset, go to the "**Quick Develop**" panel located on the right side of the screen. From there, make any necessary further modifications.

- When you are finished making changes, you should return to the Library module, pick the photographs you want to export, and then click the **Export button.** Select the appropriate settings for the file, as well as the folder in which it will be saved.

How to use the range mask feature to make selective adjustments

You can apply selected alterations to your picture in Adobe Lightroom Classic by using the range mask tool. These adjustments may be based on either the tonal range or the color range of your photograph. This is especially helpful in situations in which you want to make alterations to just certain parts of the picture rather than the whole thing as a whole. The procedure begins with establishing a range, followed by the creation of a mask based on brightness or color, and finally the application of changes to the region that was picked.

Here are the steps:

- Open Adobe Lightroom Classic and then import the picture that needs to be edited.

- Access the Develop module by selecting the "**Develop**" tab located in the upper right corner of the screen.

- Before applying the range mask to your picture, you should probably make some fundamental changes to it first, such as adjusting the exposure, contrast, or white balance.

- Make your selection from the available adjusting tools. You may be looking for the Adjustment Brush, the Graduated Filter, or the Radial Filter. You can choose the tool by either clicking on its icon or by using the corresponding keyboard shortcut (the M key for the Graduated Filter, the Shift+M key for the Radial Filter, and the K key for the Adjustment Brush).

- Create a mask over the area you want to alter by selecting it and dragging the mouse. This will be the first option you choose from.

- Access the "**Range Mask**" option by scrolling down the right panel until you reach it. To access the submenu, click the dropdown arrow.

Select either the Luminance or Color Option:

- **Luminance**: If you want to aim for a certain range of brightness, pick "**Luminance**." Move the sliders to determine the range that will be included in the mask that you are creating.

- **Color:** If you want to focus on a certain color spectrum, choose "**Color**" as your filter. After activating the color dropper tool, go to the area of the picture whose hue you want to include in the mask, and then click there. Adjust the sliders for Range and Smoothness to hone in on the perfect pick.

- After applying the range mask, you may find that your mask requires more refinement on your part. Controlling the intensity of the mask is accomplished by dragging the "**Amount**" slider.

- After you have perfected your mask, you can go on to the next step, which is to make modifications using the sliders in the right panel. These alterations will only affect the areas that are specified by your range mask going forward.

- Adjustments can be made at a finer level by using the "Before/After" view to see how the changes will look. You can also compare the original version with the changed version by using the backslash key () or by toggling the switch that is located at the bottom of the screen.

- After you have made the changes you want, you have the option of continuing to edit additional aspects of your picture or exporting the completed product.

CHAPTER EIGHT

Exporting photos from Lightroom

Classic 2024

There are many stages to exporting images from Lightroom Classic.

Here's how-to:

- Open Lightroom Classic on your PC and make sure the catalog with the images you want to export is visible.

- Proceed to the Library module and choose the images that you want to export. The Grid view allows you to see numerous photographs at once, while the Loupe view allows you to concentrate on a single image.

- After you've chosen your photos, use the keyboard shortcuts Ctrl+Shift+E (Windows) or Cmd+Shift+E (Mac) to access the menu and choose **File > Export**.

- First, choose the export destination in the Export dialog box. Select the folder on your PC where you want to save the exported images.

- The file format, color space, and quality can all be selected under the File Settings section. Typical file types include TIFF and JPEG. You can change the quality slider to suit your tastes.

- Adjust the size of your photographs under the Image Sizing section if necessary for a particular reason. If necessary, include measurements or a percentage.

- Choose whether to add metadata, such as copyright information, under the Metadata section. If you'd like, you can also decide to delete location data.

- Use the Watermarking feature to apply a watermark to your exported photos. Adjust the watermark's parameters to suit your tastes.

- Add sharpening to the exported photos under the Output Sharpening section, depending on whether the images are meant for screen or print. Adapt the configuration as necessary.

- To take further actions after exporting, go through the Export dialog's other parts, such as Post-Processing. This may include launching Adobe Photoshop or other third-party editors on the photographs.

- Save your present settings as a preset for later use if you often export pictures with the same configurations.

- Click "**Export**" after all the export settings have been specified. Lightroom Classic will begin exporting the selected images with the requested parameters to the given destination.

- Track the development in the Export Status tab of the Library module. Your exported photos will be in the designated folder after the export is finished.

How to understand the resolution

Gaining an understanding of resolution in Adobe Lightroom Classic is essential to producing high-quality picture editing output. The amount of pixels in a picture is referred to as its resolution, and it has a big impact on how crisp and high-quality the final product is.

The steps:

- Launch Adobe Lightroom Classic and bring in the images you want to edit. You can go to the Develop module for more sophisticated editing after your photos are in the Library section.

- Find the Histogram panel in the upper right section of the Develop module. You may see details about your picture, like its resolution, underneath the Histogram. Pixels are often used to indicate resolution, with examples being "**6000 x 4000**," which shows the image's width and height.

- By multiplying the width and height measurements and dividing the result by one million, the resolution may be converted to megapixels. The megapixel count, for instance, is 24 megapixels if your picture has 6000 × 4000 pixels (6000 x 4000 / 1,000,000 = 24).

- When printing or displaying your images, the resolution is quite important. Better print quality is often achieved with photographs of higher resolution. When editing photos for digital use exclusively, display size is more important than quality.

- Lightroom allows you to alter the image's size or resolution if necessary. Locate the 'Image Sizing' area on the right side of the Develop module. You can change the resolution and dimensions (width and height) here. When enlarging the size, use caution as it might result in a loss of quality.

- To inspect your picture for pixelation, enlarge it. Zooming in may make apparent pixels in your low-resolution picture, particularly if you have enlarged it. To preserve the quality of the photograph, adjust the resolution appropriately.

- You have the option to choose the export file's resolution when you export your altered picture. The export window allows you to adjust the megapixels, long edge, and short edge under the Image Sizing section. This guarantees that the final export has the appropriate resolution.

- Consider making presets in the Export dialog if you often deal with certain resolution settings. By doing this, you can preserve consistency in your exported photos and save time.

- Make sure your display is calibrated for precise editing and resolution evaluation. In particular, a calibrated monitor guarantees that the picture shown on the screen is accurate in terms of sharpness and details.

How to understand file formats

Understanding File Formats:

Raw vs. JPEG:

Raw Format:

- Unprocessed data that was taken by the camera's sensor is included in raw files.

- Since they preserve more information about the images, they provide more post-processing flexibility.

- Perfect for fine-tuning exposure, white balance, and recovering details from shadows and highlights; ideal for advanced editing.

JPEG Format:

- JPEG files undergo in-camera processing and compression.

- Less flexible in post-processing than raw, but smaller in size.

- Fit for immediate sharing or situations where storage capacity is an issue.

DNG (Digital Negative) Format:

- The exclusive raw file format used by Adobe.

- It offers an open, standardized format while being comparable to other raw formats.

- Since it's open, it might be a suitable option for long-term archiving.

TIFF (Tagged Image File Format):

- Lossless format appropriate for photos of superior quality.

- It is often used for interim file storage during intensive editing and supports layers.

PSD (Adobe Photoshop Document):

- File formats native to Adobe Photoshop.

- Allows for text, layering, and other picture changes.

- Helpful when smooth Lightroom and Photoshop interaction is needed.

Choosing Lightroom Classic 2024's Proper File Format:

Import Settings:

- Select the file format before importing.

- If you want the most editing options possible, import in raw format.

- JPEG may work well for rapid distribution or less involved editing.

Editing Workflow:

- Make extensive adjustments with raw files by using Lightroom's robust capabilities.

- If you want a standardized raw format with flexibility, think about converting to DNG.

Export Settings:

Take into account the following for final exports:

- **JPEG for Sharing**: Prepare images for sharing on websites or social media.
- **TIFF for Printing**: Preserve excellent quality while printing.
- **PSD for Additional Editing**: Photoshop is used when more work has to be done on the picture.

Archiving and Backups:

- For long-term archiving, use TIFF or DNG to preserve picture data.

- Make regular backups of the original raw files to avoid losing important data.

Performance Considerations:

- Working with raw files might cause performance issues; if you want to work more quickly without compromising editing features, think about converting to DNG.

Collaboration and Interoperability:

- Take into account file formats that are compatible with different systems and applications while working with others.

How to use the map module to geotag your photos

The steps:

- On your PC, launch **Adobe Lightroom Classic.**

- Open your Lightroom collection and import the pictures you want to geotag. This is usually accomplished using the Library module.

- Toggle between the Map and Picture Modules. The Lightroom interface has a series of modules located in the upper right corner. On the "**Map**" module, click. If it's not visible, you may need to use the keyboard shortcut "G" to activate it from the module selector.

- After accessing the Map module, a global map ought to appear. If you have any photographs with GPS coordinates already contained in the metadata, Lightroom will attempt to locate them on a map automatically. If not, you may manually drag and drop images onto the map to reposition them where they belong.

- Add GPS Coordinates (if needed): You can manually add GPS coordinates if they are missing from your photos.
- ➢ In the filmstrip at the bottom, choose the pictures you want to geotag.
- ➢ Right-click on the location of the picture shoot on the map.
- ➢ From the context menu, choose "**Add GPS Coordinates to Selected Photos**".

- **Adjust GPS Coordinates (if needed):** Drag and drop the images into the map to change the location if the automated placing is off.

- You must make sure that any changes you make to the GPS coordinates are saved to the metadata after adding or updating them. To do this, either select the "Save Metadata" button in the Library module, or use "**Ctrl + S**" on a Windows computer, or "Cmd + S" on a Mac.

- Browse your photos depending on their geographic location by using the Map module. You can see the images taken in a certain region by clicking on a spot on the map.

How to create slideshows and web galleries

Creating Slideshows in Adobe Lightroom Classic:

- To add photos to your slideshow, open Adobe Lightroom Classic and import the desired pictures.

- For easier administration, group your images into collections if needed.

- Open the Develop module and do any required picture edits, such as cropping, adjusting the color, or adding filters.

- Click the Slideshow tab in the upper-right panel to get to the Slideshow module.

- Select a slideshow template and layout. The text overlays, backdrop color, and arrangement are all customizable.

- To include background music in your presentation, go to the Music panel and choose the desired audio file.

- Modify the Slideshow module's transition settings from slide to slide. You may add pan and zoom effects, change the transition type, and adjust the length.

- Add text overlays to provide details on every picture. In the Text Overlay panel, change the font's size, location, and style.

- To preview the appearance of your slideshow, click the **Preview button**. Make any required changes to the transitions, timing, or other parameters.

- After you're happy with your slideshow, export it in the format of your choice by clicking the Export PDF or Export Video option.

Creating Web Galleries in Adobe Lightroom Classic:

- Use the Library module to import and arrange your picture collection. To get a more efficient process, think about establishing collections.

- Click the Web tab in the top-right panel to get to the Web module.

- From the Template Browser on the left, choose a web gallery template. Lightroom Classic offers a range of settings to suit diverse needs and aesthetic preferences.

- Using the options in the right panel, modify the look of your online gallery. Make changes to the fonts, colors, and layout to suit your tastes.

- Configure settings unique to your site, such as the title, metadata, and export choices. Make sure you adjust the gallery settings to suit your tastes.

- To see the preview of your online gallery, click the **Preview** in Browser option. See if anything needs to be adjusted.

- After you're happy, choose **Export Site**. Select the export parameters and destination folder. For your online gallery, Lightroom Classic will create the HTML files and related components.

- You may immediately post the exported web gallery if you have your web server. If not, you can upload it to your favorite hosting site or use a third-party service.

How to use the book module to create photo books

Creating a Photo Book in Adobe Lightroom Classic:

Here are the steps:

- Open **Adobe Lightroom Classic 2024** and import the images into the Library section of your photo book.

- Select the "**Book**" module from the interface's upper right panel.

- Choose the kind of book you wish to generate (Blurb, PDF, or JPEG) in the Book module. Depending on whatever version of Lightroom Classic you have, the options could change

- Change the pre-made book layouts in Lightroom Classic. Select a layout style based on what you like.

- There's a panel with a filmstrip of your images on the left. To add pictures to your book, drag & drop them into the centrally located pages.

- Choose a page and edit it using the options on the right. You have more options to alter picture size, add text, and modify the layout.

- The Text panel allows you to include text or captions in your picture book. As required, adjust the text, size, and color.

- To adjust page order, add or delete pages, and add page numbers, use the Page panel.

- Press the "**Preview**" button to examine the layout of your picture book. This assists you in making any required changes before completing the book.

- After you are happy with your picture book, if you choose the Blurb option, you can purchase a physical copy straight from Blurb or export it as a PDF or JPEG for printing at a photo lab.

- Save your picture book project before exiting Lightroom so you can revisit it and make any necessary edits later.

- To submit your project and finish the order, adhere to the on-screen instructions if you're printing with Blurb.

How to use the print module to create prints and contact sheets

The steps:

- Go to the **Library module** in Adobe Lightroom Classic after opening it.

- Choose which pictures to use for your contact sheet or print.

- To access the Print module, choose the "**Print**" tab located at the top of the screen.

- The "**Layout Style**" panel is located on the right. Select the desired layout style, such as Contact Sheet/Single Image.

- Depending on your desired result, adjust the "**Image Settings**" panel's Cell Size, Resolution, and other variables.

- In the "**Page**" panel, modify the Page settings. The paper size, orientation, and other page-related parameters may be adjusted here.

- Go to the "**Print Job**" panel by navigating. The printer, paper type, and quality settings may all be adjusted here.

- Select "**Printer**" or "**JPEG File**" to save as an image file from the "Print to" dropdown menu to get a preview of your print or contact sheet.

- Make adjustments using the "**Page**" and "**Print Job**" panels. If necessary, you may add watermarks, change the margins, or apply print sharpening.

- Click "**Print**" to send the job to your printer or save it as an image file when you are happy with the settings.

- Once printed or saved, go over the outcomes. Return to the Print module and make the necessary modifications there if they are required.

CHAPTER NINE

Creating Photo Books with Lightroom Classic 2024

How to make slideshows in the slideshow module

Here are the steps:

- Open Adobe Lightroom Classic on your computer by opening up the Adobe Lightroom Classic program.

- Import and Organize your Photos. Do this by going into your Lightroom library and importing the images that you want to include in your slideshow. If you haven't done so before, you should have them organized in the Library module.

- Navigate to the Slideshow Module by Clicking on the "**Slideshow**" Module in the Module Picker at the Top of the Page. It seems to be a rectangle with a triangle embedded inside it.

- In the Filmstrip at the bottom of the screen, choose the photos that you would want to include in your slideshow.

- On the right panel of the Slideshow module, you'll discover many options to choose from to personalize your presentation. This covers choices such as Layout, Backdrop, Overlays, and Playback. Make the necessary adjustments so that they correspond to your tastes. You also have the option of selecting a pre-made template from the Template Browser to the left of the screen.

- The Layout panel gives you the ability to change the appearance of each slide individually. You have many options available to you for including features like text, identification plates, and numerous other components in your presentations.

- Navigate to the panel labeled "**Music**" if you wish to include music in your presentation. In this section, you can choose the music you want to listen to, change the level, and make any other necessary adjustments to the audio settings.

- In the Playback panel, you may change the length of time that each slide is shown. You also have the option to choose various settings associated with the playback, such as whether or not to include a title screen for the slide show.

- To obtain a preview of how your slideshow will appear, click the "**Preview**" button located at the bottom of the screen. You are now able to make any required modifications thanks to this.

- When you have finished customizing your slideshow to your liking, you can then export it. You can export your slideshow as a video file by clicking the "Export Video" button, or you can generate a PDF of it by clicking the "Export PDF" button.

- If you want to, you may save your slideshow and then share it with other people. Depending on what you want, you have the option of saving it as either a video file or a PDF.

How to add text and captions to your

photo book

Here are the steps:

- Open the Adobe Lightroom Classic application on your PC. Make sure that the most recent version of the program is installed on your computer.

- You should import the photos that you want to use in your photo book into the library of your Lightroom Classic software if you have not already done so. If you want the procedure to go more smoothly, organize the items into collections or folders.

- While in the Library module, go to the panel on the left and click the "**Book**" module.

- To begin work on a new book project, choose the "**Create Saved Book**" option from the menu.

- You will be able to see the layout of your picture book via the Book module. You have options on the right side of the screen to choose a book type, make adjustments to the layout, and a few other things.

- Drag your photos from the Filmstrip at the bottom of the screen onto the appropriate pages to include them in the book. You can reorder them by dragging and dropping them into a new position.

Add Text and Captions

- Navigate to the page on which you want to add text and click there.

- Move to the "**Text**" panel that is located in the right panel. You will find options to add a page number, picture text, and a photo description in this section.

- Select the "**Photo Text**" box and click on it to write a caption. After that, you will be able to fill in your caption.

- Personalize the text by making changes to the font, size, and color, in addition to the other available formatting choices in the Text panel.

- If you want to add captions or text to additional pages, repeat this method for each of those pages.

- Once you are satisfied with the way the writing and captions look in your picture book, you can preview it by clicking on the "**Book**" dropdown menu and choosing "**Preview This Book.**"

- Check that the layout, the text, and the captions are all presented in the manner that you like.

- You can export your picture book after you have completed it to your satisfaction. In the Book module, choose the "**Book Settings**" option to make changes.

- Configure your export settings, including the resolution and file type of the exported file.

- To make a PDF version of your picture book, you must first choose the "**Export Book to PDF**" option.

Check Your Work and Print It Out

- Open your photo book in the produced PDF format to evaluate it.

- If you are pleased with it, you have the option of printing it via the printing provider of your choice or saving it for digital distribution.

How to use auto layout to automate your layout process

Using Auto Layout in Adobe Lightroom Classic:

Adobe Lightroom Classic has tools called Auto Layout that may assist in automating the process of arranging and organizing your photographs.

Here are the steps:

- Launch Adobe Lightroom Classic, and then go to the Library module to import your photographs.

- Ensure that your photos are arranged in the Catalog in an orderly fashion and properly tagged with relevant information and keywords.

- Navigate to the Library section of the platform by selecting the "**Library**" tab located in the upper left-hand corner of the display.

- To switch to the Grid view, hit "**G**" on your keyboard or select the Grid symbol in the toolbar. Both of these options are available.

- Navigate to the Library module's toolbar and look for the Auto Layout choices there.

- Adobe may have incorporated sophisticated auto-layout technologies, however, this depends on the version and any upgrades that have been applied. Keep an eye out for phrases such as "**Auto Arrange**" and "**Smart Layout**."

- Move to the options or settings that are associated with the Auto Layout feature.

- Adjust the options for the layout, including the distance between photographs, the size of the grid, and any other preferences you may have. This assists in personalizing the auto-layout following your preferences.

- Using the auto-layout feature, choose the photos you want to organize in the desired manner. You have the option of manually selecting photographs, or you may limit your options by using filters and flags.

- To use the auto layout function, either use the keyboard shortcut linked with it or click on the icon labeled "**Auto Layout**." By performing this step, Lightroom will be prompted to automatically organize the chosen photographs following the layout settings that have been provided.

- Once the auto layout has been applied, check the arrangement and make any required revisions.

- Manual adjustments are often supported in Adobe Lightroom Classic, which means you may use the drag-and-drop functionality to move photographs as required.

- When you reach a point where you are content with the layout, you should think about preserving it or synchronizing it across many photos if you have a certain arrangement in mind for a collection of pictures.

- Once you have finished customizing your layout, you can export your photos or instantly share them using Lightroom Classic.

How to customize your background

Follow the steps below to customize your background:

- Launch Adobe Lightroom Classic and then import the picture that needs to be edited into the program.

- To access the Develop module, either hit the "**D**" key on your keyboard or select the "**Develop**" tab located in the upper right corner of the screen.

- The Basic settings are located in the panel on the right-hand side of the screen. To improve the quality of your photograph, make the necessary adjustments to the exposure, contrast, highlights, shadows, whites, and blacks.

- To crop your picture and make adjustments to the composition, use the Crop Overlay tool (keyboard shortcut: R). Make sure your subject is appropriately framed.

- To make fine-tuned adjustments to the colors in your picture, go to the HSL/Color panel. You can make adjustments to the colors, saturation, and brightness thanks to this.

- To apply a gradient effect to your picture, use the Gradient Filter tool by pressing the M key on your keyboard. Using this tool, you may make adjustments to the background independently from the adjustments you make to the foreground. Move the filter to the position where you want the effect to be, then make any necessary adjustments to the parameters, such as the exposure, color balance, or temperature.

- You can paint changes onto specified regions using the Adjustment Brush (keyboard shortcut: K). Use it to make selective changes to the backdrop by boosting or lowering the intensity of selected parts.

- To give your picture a unique appearance, you should investigate the Effects tab, where you may find choices such as vignettes and grain. By darkening the boundaries of the vignette, one may call attention to the topic that is being shown.

- More sophisticated tonal changes can be made using the panel labeled "**Tone Curve**." You may modify the contrast and tone of your picture by creating a custom curve in your image editing software.

- If you are preparing the picture for print or a particular display, you may wish to utilize the Soft Proofing option to simulate how the colors will appear in various output situations. This can be done by clicking the "**Image**" menu and selecting **"Prepare for Print" or "Prepare for Specific Displays."**

- If you have finished making changes to the picture, and you are ready to save it, click on the "**Export**" button. Determine the correct parameters for the file, as well as its location.

- To evaluate the results of your modifications, use the "Y" key to go back and forth between the unaltered and modified versions of the document.

- Create a preset for a certain style if you use that style regularly and store the parameters to use in the future.

How to design your book cover

Follow the steps below to design your book cover:

- Before you begin, gather all the components you want to include in your book cover, such as photos, text, and any other visuals. This should be done before you start designing the cover. To maintain an air of professionalism, check to see that these materials have a good resolution.

- Then proceed to launch Adobe Photoshop on your computer.

- Go to the File menu and pick the **New option** to start a new document. Adjust the measurements so that they correspond to the size of the book cover that you want (if it's a printed book, also take into account the trim size, bleed, and spine width).

- Select a color for the background or a picture to use. You can either import a picture and resize it to cover the canvas using the Paint Bucket tool, or you can use the Paint Bucket tool to fill the background layer.

- Drag your primary photos onto the canvas and then choose **File > Place Embedded** from the menu bar. Modify their dimensions and placement as required.

- Experiment with different blending modes, which can be found in the Layers panel, to get the look you want.

- Select the Text tool, and then select a typeface that is appropriate for the genre and subject matter of your book.

- On the cover, write the book's title, the author's name, and any additional information you'd want to include.

- To improve the legibility of the text, try experimenting with text effects such as drop shadows and gradients.

- Import any other visual assets that you may need, such as icons, logos, or ornamental elements.

- Make adjustments to their size, location, and opacity so that the design as a whole looks better.

- To fine-tune the colors, contrast, and saturation of your design, use adjustment layers, which can be located in the Layers panel in Adobe Photoshop.

- To add a more creative touch, play around with different filters and effects.

- Make sure to save your project as a PSD file so that any layers may be accessed and edited later.

- Export either a version with high quality for printing or a version optimized for the web if the cover is for an electronic book.

- Show your design to other people to receive their comments on it. Think about the feedback you may get from prospective readers or colleagues working in the publishing sector.

- Consider the comments provided and make any required improvements.

- Save the finished version or export it in the needed format (JPEG, PNG, etc.) for the publishing platform that you use.

CHAPTER TEN

Converting RAW files to DNG

Follow the steps below to convert RAW files to DNG:

- On your PC, launch Adobe Lightroom Classic 2024. To use the newest features and enhancements, make sure you have the most recent version installed.

- In the Library module, choose **File > Import Photos and Video** or click the "**Import**" button. Find the folder where your RAW files are stored, then choose to import them. During this phase, you may also modify import options like file organization and metadata.

- Once imported, find the photos you want to convert to DNG by navigating to the Library module. If you want to choose a range, click the first picture, then hold down the **Shift** key and click the final image. As an alternative, you may click on individual photographs to choose non-contiguous ones while holding down the Ctrl/Cmd key.

- Click the **Library module icon** in the upper left corner of the screen to switch to the Library module.

- You can make any required edits in the Develop module before converting to DNG. Although it's not required, here is the location to make any simple updates or corrections.

- Go to **Library > Convert Photos to DNG** in the Library module while the chosen photos are still there. As an alternative, you can use the context menu to choose "Convert to DNG" when you right-click on the chosen photos.

The dialog box labeled "Convert Photos" will show up. You may adjust several settings here:

- **Location**: Select the destination for the DNG files that have been converted.

- **File Handling**: Choose how you want to handle the converted original RAW files.

- **File Naming**: Assign the transformed files a naming scheme.

- **Embed Fast Load Data**: This feature may help certain programs load photos more quickly.

- **Option to Embed Original Raw File**: Select whether you want to include the original RAW file in the DNG file.

- After adjusting the settings to suit your tastes, press the "**Convert**" button. The chosen RAW files will begin to be converted to DNG format by Lightroom.

- Once the conversion process is finished, the DNG files are located in the designated directory. It is a good idea to check that the converted files live up to your expectations.

How to understand tone curve adjustments

Adobe Lightroom Classic has a useful feature called the Tone Curve that lets photographers adjust the contrast and tone of their photos. It gives you a visual depiction of how the tones in your shot are distributed, from highlights to shadows.

Understand tone curve adjustments:

- Open Adobe Lightroom Classic and import the desired picture for editing.

- Use the keyboard shortcut **'D'** to access the Develop module or select the Develop tab located in the upper right corner of the screen.

- Locate the **'Tone Curve'** tab in the panel on the right. It may be found under the Histogram.

- A graph with a diagonal line extending from the bottom-left to the top-right corner is shown in the Tone Curve panel. *(NB: The original tonal values of your picture are represented by this line).*

- The input tonal values are represented by the horizontal axis, which runs from highlights on the right to shadows on the left. The output tonal values are represented by the vertical axis, which runs from dark at the bottom to brilliant at the top.

Basic Tone Curve Adjustments

Point Curve Presets:

- Presets for typical tone curve modifications are available in Lightroom. To access choices such as Linear, Medium Contrast, and Strong Contrast, click on the **'Point Curve'** dropdown menu.

Dragging Points:

- The tone curve can be adjusted by dragging and clicking on different tonal areas. Pulling down the tones darkens them while pulling up the brightness intensifies them.

Mastering the Tone Curve

RGB Channels:

- By choosing the Red, Green, and Blue color channels from the drop-down menu above the tone curve, you can modify each one separately.

Contrast S-Curve:

- Enhancing contrast by elevating the midpoint and adding a point in the highlights and shadows creates an 'S-curve'. This is a popular method for giving a picture more impact.

Fine-Tuning:

- To make little changes, use many points. Concentrate on certain areas of the curve to fine-tune various tone ranges.

Using the Targeted Adjustment Tool

Targeted Adjustment Tool:

- To modify individual tonal sections of your picture, click and drag the target icon in the

Tone Curve panel. Precise modifications are possible with this interactive technique, which is intuitive.

Before and After

Preview your Changes:

- Alternate between the before and after views by toggling the 'Y' key. This aids in the assessment of the effects of your tone curve modifications.

Final Adjustments

Check Other Settings:

- To guarantee a well-balanced overall appearance, check additional parameters like exposure, contrast, and saturation after making modifications to the tone curve.

Save your Work

Presets and History

- If your changes are satisfactory, you may want to save your configurations as a preset for later use. If necessary, you may also review your editing history.

How to back up and restore your

Lightroom Classic Catalog

Backing Up Your Lightroom Classic Catalog:

- On your PC, launch Adobe Lightroom Classic 2024.

- Make sure your Lightroom catalog is consistent before generating a backup. Optimizing the catalog to get rid of any extraneous information is a smart strategy. Go to **File > Optimize Catalog** to do this.

- On your computer, your Lightroom catalog is normally kept in the "**Pictures**" or "**Photos**" folder.

- Look for the "**Lightroom**" folder and locate your catalog file (which has a.lrcat extension).

Select Backup Preferences:

➢ On Windows, choose **Edit > Catalog Settings**; on Mac, select **Lightroom Classic > Catalog Settings**.

➢ Find the "**Backup**" section under the General tab.

➢ Turn on "**When Lightroom next exits**" to have Lightroom create a backup the next time you shut it down.

- Select **File > Back Up Catalog** to start creating a backup right now. This is helpful before making big adjustments or importing an excessive amount of images.

- To start the backup process, close Lightroom Classic.

Restoring Your Lightroom Classic Catalog:

The steps:

- Open the folder containing your Lightroom catalog.

- Locate the "**Backups**" folder, which has dated subfolders containing backups of your catalog.

- Decide which backup you want to recover. To get the most current modifications, it is advised to use the most recent backup.

- Make a copy of the selected backup folder and put it in the directory containing your Lightroom catalog.

- Replace the current catalog file (which has the.lrcat extension) with "**YourCatalogName_old.lrcat**."

- Change the name of the backup catalog file to the same as the original.

- Open Lightroom Classic

- The repaired catalog needs to be recognized automatically. If not, find and access the recovered catalog by using **File > Access Catalog**.

- Confirm that all of your images and adjustments are still there. You may need to reconnect any photos that seem to be missing by finding the missing files.

CHAPTER ELEVEN

Working with Local Adjustments

(Graduated Filter, Brush, Radial Filter)

Graduated Filter:

- Open your photo in Adobe Lightroom Classic's Develop module.

- To use the Graduated Filter tool, locate it on the Develop module toolbar or click the 'M' key on your keyboard.

- To change an area, click and drag it across it. Gradients are produced by the filter's progressive application of its effect. The filter can be resized and repositioned as necessary.

- To fine-tune the chosen area, play about with the Gradient Filter panel's settings for Exposure, Contrast, Highlights, Shadows, and more.

- To further fine-tune the filter's effects according to color or brightness, use the Range Mask option.

Brush Tool:

- To use the Brush tool, find it on the Develop module toolbar or use the keypad shortcut **'K'**.

- Apply paint to the precise areas that need modification. The square bracket keys '[' and ']' on the left and right may be used to change the brush size.

- The areas you painted are indicated by the overlay.

- Modify the Brush panel's exposure, temperature, clarity, and other variables.

- To selectively erase brush modifications, use the Erase option.

Radial Filter:

- Activate the Radial Filter tool by pressing **'Shift+M'** or locate it in the Develop module toolbar.

- To design a circular or elliptical filter, click and drag. You can choose to make the modifications outside or within the filter.

- Adjust the filter's size and location as necessary.

- To alter parameters like exposure, contrast, and other settings comparable to the Graduated Filter, use the Radial Filter panel.

- Try alternating between inner and outside changes by experimenting with the Invert Mask option.

Advanced Retouching Techniques

Beyond simple tweaks, advanced retouching uses complex methods to enhance details and provide a polished appearance.

Here are the steps:

Library Module Organization

Be sure your library is organized before you start retouching. Use star ratings, flags, and keywords to quickly classify and identify photos. When using sophisticated retouching methods, this will save time.

Develop Module Basics:

Start with simple tweaks in the Develop module, such as exposure, contrast, and color correction. These tweaks provide a strong starting point for more complex retouching.

Advanced Spot Removal:

- **Healing Brush:** To erase blemishes, spots, or defects, use the Healing Brush. For fine control, change the feathering and brush size.

- **Clone Stamp:** This tool works well for copying a particular area. When you want to change a texture or item, this is helpful.

Graduated and Radial Filters:

- **Graduated Filter**: Use the Graduated Filter to bring out certain details in a picture. For instance, make a scene cozier or the sky darker.

- **Radial Filter:** This filter lets you make changes in an ellipse or circular form, much like the Graduated Filter. This works well for bringing a topic or vignette to life.

Adjustment Brush for Localized Editing:

One effective tool for targeted modifications is the Adjustment Brush. It may be used to add selective sharpness, whiten teeth, and improve eyesight. For even more precision, use the range mask tool and apply precise brushstrokes.

HSL and Color Grading:

Use the Hue, Saturation, and Luminance (HSL) tab to adjust certain colors in your picture. With color grading, you can create a more theatrical effect by changing the hues of the highlights, midtones, and shadows.

Detail Panel for Noise Reduction and Sharpening:

The Detail panel is crucial for enhancing your image's clarity. When enhancing details, use the Sharpening sliders with caution. When reducing unwanted noise, particularly in low light, use the Noise Reduction settings.

Advanced Lens Corrections:

A sleek, polished appearance is achieved by correcting lens distortions. Take care of problems like distortion, vignetting, and chromatic aberration in the Lens Corrections panel.

Profiles and Presets:

Create and use presets for your favorite retouching techniques to save time. Try out many profiles to see which one best suits your image.

Exporting for Different Platforms:

Think about the platform that will be used to show your image. To guarantee the best possible quality for social media, print, or the web, modify the export parameters appropriately.

Advanced color correction and grading techniques

Here are the steps:

- In Lightroom Classic, import your photos first.

- To arrange your photos into folders or collections, use the Library module.

- Use any flags, keywords, or information that are required for effective sorting.

- To start the color-correcting procedure, go to the Develop module.

- Begin with fundamental changes such as contrast, exposure, highlights, shadows, whites, and blacks.

- Make sure the tone range is well-balanced before adjusting the color.

- Use the White Balance tool to fix any problems with color temperature.

- Modify the tint and temperature sliders to get a balanced color temperature.

- Adjust the white balance according to the illumination during the picture session.

- To change a particular color, go to the HSL/Color panel.

- Modify each color channel's hue, saturation, and luminance. This gives you the ability to modify and improve certain colors in your picture.

- To get exact control over contrast and color balance, use the Tone Curve.

- To keep the RGB curve balanced overall, use anchor points.

- To achieve delicate color changes, independently adjust the Red, Green, and Blue channels.

- Use split toning to improve the image's overall mood.

- Apply varying tones to the highlights and shadows to get a stylish or cinematic effect.

- Steer clear of an excessively exaggerated look by maintaining a modest balance.

- To make small but significant changes to the overall color rendering, use the Calibration panel.

- To get the appropriate color cast, adjust the main hues of red, green, and blue.

- Use radial and graduated filters sparingly to adjust color and exposure in certain areas.

- Use the Adjustment Brush to fine-tune color corrections via local changes.

- Apply paint over certain areas to adjust sharpness, color, or exposure. This makes targeted and in-depth color grading possible.

- To see how your photo will appear printed or on various screens, use the Soft Proofing option.

- Modify hues and tones so that the finished product reflects your artistic intent.

- To keep your editing perspective intact, take pauses during the process.

- Go over your changes again, enlarge for a closer look at each pixel, and make any necessary corrections.

- Export your photo in the format and quality of your choice when you're happy with the color adjustments and grading.

How to use the transform panel for perspective correction

- To edit a picture, use **Adobe Lightroom Classic** and import it into your collection.

- Press "D" on your keyboard to enter the "**Develop**" module, or select the "**Develop**" tab located in the upper-right corner of the screen.

- The "**Transform**" panel is located in the Develop module on the right-hand side. Toggle it on by pressing "T" if it's not visible.

- There are several correcting options in the Transform section. The Three Fundamentals: Manual, Guided, and Upright. Select the setting that best meets your requirements for correction.

Upright Mode

Upright has preset sub-modes:

➢ **Auto**: Uses perspective to try to automatically level and straighten the picture.

➢ **Level**: Ensures that the picture is level.

➢ **Vertical**: Adjusts vertical viewpoint.

➢ Full: Makes both vertical and level adjustments.

• If you choose Guided, click the "**Guided**" option and then drag the cursor along the two straight lines. Lightroom will make the appropriate perspective adjustments.

Manual Adjustments

To make exact modifications, use the sliders located under the "**Manual**" tab:

➢ **Vertical**: Vertically modifies perspective.

➢ **Horizontal**: Modifies the viewpoint's horizontal alignment.

➢ **Rotate**: Turns the picture around.

➢ **Aspect**: Modifies the ratio of aspect.

- Turning on "**Constrain to Crop**" will guarantee that the adjustments you make won't leave empty spaces around the picture.

- After making the necessary guided manual or automated modifications, use the sliders to fine-tune the picture until the appropriate perspective is achieved.

- Depending on the adjustments performed, you may have to crop the picture to get rid of any voids around the edges.

- Press the backslash key ("") to examine the before-and-after view, or use the "Y" key to compare the altered version with the original.

- Click "**Done**" or go on to another module if you're happy. Go to the Library module and continue with the export settings if you're ready to export.

How to understand and use split toning

Understanding Split Toning

Split toning means adding distinct hues to an image's highlights and shadows. Depending on the hues and levels of intensity used, this may have a subtle or striking impact.

Highlights and Shadows:

- **Highlights**: The areas of a picture that stand out the most, such as the sky or reflecting surfaces.

- **Shadows**: The darker portions, such as the corners or shadowed sections.

Hue, Saturation, and Balance:

- **Hue**: The actual color, such as yellow or blue.

- **Saturation**: The color's intensity.

- **Balance**: Modifies the proportions of the outlined and shaded regions.

How to Use Split Toning

The steps:

- Import your picture into Lightroom Classic.

- Click on the "**Develop**" module on the upper right.

- Find the Split Toning Panel. It's located under the "Basic" tab in the right-hand panel.

- Before split toning, verify your white balance is adjusted accordingly.

- Increase the "**Saturation**" slider for the highlights.

- Choose a color using the "**Hue**" slider.

- Make the shadows' "**Saturation**" higher.

- Choose a new hue using the "**Hue**" slider.

- Use the "**Balance**" slider to modify the balance between highlights and shadows. Move it left for more highlights, and right for more shadows.

- Adjust the overall intensity of the split toning effect using the "**Saturation**" sliders for both highlights and shadows.

- Toggle the split toning panel on/off to observe the before-and-after effect.

- Play around with various color schemes and saturations.

- Refine until you obtain the desired appearance.

- After you're happy, you can save your split toning configuration as a preset for later use.

- Complete your editing process with further tweaks like exposure, contrast, or sharpness.

- Once happy with the adjustments, export your picture.

Tips:

- **Subtle vs. bold**: While dramatic selections may provide a styled or retro appearance, subtle tweaks can accentuate natural tones.

- **Consistency**: For a coherent effect, split toning should be applied consistently throughout a collection of images.

- **Experiment**: To discover the ideal mixture, don't be afraid to try out various colors, saturations, and balances.

CHAPTER TWELVE

Advanced Techniques

How to create and use virtual copies

One of Lightroom Classic's most useful features is the ability to create and use virtual clones, which let you try out various modifications without compromising the original picture. Virtual copies don't take up extra disk space on your computer; they are just replicas of your photos stored in Lightroom.

Here's how to create virtual copies:

- Turn on your computer and open the Adobe Lightroom Classic program.

- Add the pictures to your Lightroom collection that you want to work with.

- Choose the picture that you want to make a virtual clone of from the Library or Develop module.

- Select "**Photo**" from the menu.

- Select the option "**Create Virtual Copy**."

The chosen picture will be converted to a virtual copy and shown on the filmstrip at the bottom of the screen.

Using Virtual Copies:

- Click on the virtual copy in the filmstrip to choose it.

- To make changes, go to the Develop module. Modify exposure, contrast, colors, and other elements without compromising the original picture.

- The Develop module makes it simple to compare the adjustments made to the virtual copy and the original.

- You can undo any adjustments on a virtual copy by right-clicking on the picture and choosing "**Develop Settings**" > "**Reset**."

- You can categorize and differentiate between virtual copies using flags, stars, or color labels.

- You have the option to save several versions of a picture by exporting either the original or any of its virtual duplicates.

- If you want to get rid of a virtual duplicate without getting rid of the original picture, you may right-click on it and choose "**Remove Photo**" > "**Delete from Disk**" or "**Remove**."

Tips:

Non-Destructive Editing:

- Keep in mind that Lightroom allows for non-destructive adjustments on any images, including the original. Virtual replicas provide an extra degree of adaptability.

Versioning Snapshot:

- Use the "**Create Snapshot**" function in the Develop module to take a snapshot of a specific edit state.

Keywords and Metadata:

- Metadata and keywords from the original picture are carried over to virtual copies, simplifying management and image search.

How to use the Dehaze slider

Here are the steps:

- Open Adobe Lightroom Classic and open the picture you want to edit.

- Click the "**Develop**" tab in the upper right corner to access the "**Develop**" module once the picture has been imported.

- The Develop module has many panels on the right side. The Dehaze slider is located in the "**Basic**" panel.

- Navigate down to the "**Effects**" area in the Basic panel. You'll find the "**Dehaze**" slider in this area.

- To enhance or decrease the dehazing effect, move the Dehaze slider to the right or left. The slider helps to cut through atmospheric haze or fog in your shot by increasing or decreasing the contrast in the highlights and mid-tones.

- You may want to modify additional sliders in addition to the Dehaze slider, depending on your picture. To get the desired overall appearance, for instance, you may need to adjust the exposure, contrast, or clarity.

- Press and hold the keyboard's "Y" key to examine a side-by-side comparison of the before and after. This enables you to evaluate the effects of your modifications.

- Gradually implementing the Dehaze effect is often more successful than making drastic changes. This is particularly true if you're going for a result that seems natural.

- You can use the masking tools to apply the Dehaze effect selectively. In the toolbar under the histogram, choose the "**Brush**" tool.

Next, select "**Dehaze**" from the "**Effect**" dropdown menu. Now, you can apply the Dehaze effect to certain regions of your picture.

- After making any necessary revisions and dehazing adjustments, you can export your picture by clicking on the "**File**" menu and choosing "**Export**."

Tips and tricks for using the Calibration pane

Adobe Lightroom Classic's Calibration window is essential for adjusting how well your photos display in terms of color. It enables you to subtly alter the main colors of your images, changing the way they seem and feel overall.

To get the most out of the Calibration pane, follow these tips:

Accessing the Calibration Window

- Launch **Adobe Lightroom Classic** and import the picture you want to edit.

- Click the **Develop tab** or hit 'D' on your keyboard to access the Develop module.

Find the Calibration Pane

- In the right-hand panel of the Develop module, the Calibration window is normally found near the bottom.

- It is labeled "**Camera Calibration.**"

Understanding the Sliders

- There are three sliders in the Calibration pane: Red Primary, Green Primary, and Blue Primary.

- The intensity of the appropriate color in the picture is adjusted using these sliders.

Fine-Tuning Colors

- To change the image's red tone strength, use the Red Primary slider.

- Green tones are influenced by the Green Primary slider, whereas blue tones are influenced by the Blue Primary slider.

Balancing Skin Tones

- Take note of skin tones while working on portraiture. To get skin hues that seem realistic, adjust the Red Primary.

- Adjust the Green Primary to correct any skin color casts that you do not want.

Achieving a Desired Look

- Try adjusting the three sliders in various ways to get the right color balance.

- The Calibration pane lets you make artistic edits that give your images a distinctive appearance.

Resetting Adjustments

- Use the **Reset button** in the lower right corner of the Develop module or double-click on any slider to start again or reverse your modifications.

Syncing Calibration Settings

- To achieve a unified appearance across several photographs, you may synchronize the calibration settings if you have a collection of shots taken in comparable situations.

Monitoring Histogram Changes

- Observe the histogram while making modifications. Make sure that none of your adjustments cause the highlights or shadows to clip or lose detail.

Saving Custom Calibration Profiles

- If you work with a certain style often, you can save your personalized Calibration settings as a profile for later use.

How to use the calibration pane

One option in Lightroom Classic that lets you tweak the color and tone of your photos is the calibration pane.

Here's how to use the calibration pane:

- First, launch Lightroom Classic.

- Open the Lightroom Classic library and import the picture you want to modify.

- Click the "**Develop**" tab in the upper-right corner of the screen to get to the "**Develop**" module.

- Locate the panels on the right-hand side of the "**Develop**" module. Once you reach the "**Camera Calibration**" section, scroll down. Usually, it may be found toward the bottom of the panel on the right.

Usually, the Calibration window has sliders that let you change the image's main colors. Typical sliders include:

o **Red Primary**: Modifies the red tones' color.
o The **Green Primary** tone modifies the color of green tones.

o **Blue Primary**: Modifies the blue tones' color.

o **Hue Saturation**: Adjusts how saturated certain color ranges are.

o **Saturation**: Modifies the image's overall saturation.

o **Luminance**: Regulates the hues of various color spectrums.

- To modify the colors of your picture, use the sliders. For instance, you may play with the Blue Primary slider to intensify the blue tones in the sky. You can adjust the Red Primary slider if you think your image's red tones are too strong.

- Keep an eye on the picture preview in the main editing window while you make changes. A real-time preview of the image's alterations is offered by Lightroom Classic.

- Since calibration is a subjective process, the best settings may differ based on your tastes and the particulars of the image. To get the right appearance, take your time adjusting the sliders and watching how they change.

- After you're happy with the calibration tweaks, you can export the picture or carry out other editing operations.

- Lightroom Classic allows you to share or export a picture once you've made all the necessary modifications.

How to work with HDR and Panorama merges

The steps:

- To begin the HDR merging, open Adobe Lightroom Classic and import the bracketed images you want to use.

- Choose the Library module and the pictures you want to combine. To capture a greater dynamic range, a sequence of photos with varying exposure values should be taken.

- To merge to HDR, select the **'Develop'** tab to get to the Develop module.

- After you've chosen the photos you want to combine, right-click and choose **"Photo Merge" > "HDR."**

- The window for the HDR Merge Preview will open. The photos will be automatically aligned by Lightroom, and any ghosting from moving subjects will be eliminated. Modify the parameters as necessary:

  o **Auto Align:** Make sure the photos are aligned by selecting this option.

  o **Auto Settings**: Lightroom's analysis allows it to make automated tone changes. Moreover, you have the option to use your settings.

- Press **'Merge'** to begin the HDR merging procedure. The combined HDR picture will be saved as a new DNG file in Lightroom.

- The Develop module allows you to make further edits to the picture once the HDR merging is finished. To get the desired effect, play about with the exposure, contrast, color, and other variables.

Panorama Merge in Adobe Lightroom Classic 2024:

The steps:

- Open the set of images that you want to combine into a panoramic.

- Choose **'Photo Merge' > 'Panorama'** with a right-click after selecting the pictures.

- The window for the Panorama Merge Preview will open. Depending on your desire, choose a projection type (Perspective, Cylindrical, or Spherical).
  o **Auto Settings:** Lightroom can make automated tone changes.
  o **Boundary Warp:** Use this slider to fill in the panorama's boundaries automatically.

- Press **'Merge'** to begin the panoramic merging procedure. The combined panorama will be saved as a new DNG file in Lightroom.

- The Develop section allows you to further edit the panorama after merging. To improve the picture, play about with the exposure, white balance, and clarity settings.

- After you're OK with your adjustments, select **'Export'** from the **'File'** menu to export the HDR or panoramic picture.

- Select the export options, including the destination folder, file type, and resolution.

Advanced export options for printing and web output

The steps:

- Open Adobe Lightroom Classic. Make sure you have chosen the catalog that contains the photos you want to export when you launch Lightroom Classic.

- Select the photos you want to export from the Library module. Holding down the **Ctrl (Windows) or Command (Mac) key** while clicking on one picture allows you to choose numerous photos.

- Open the Export Dialog by selecting "**Export**" from the "**File**" menu (or by using the keyboard shortcut **Ctrl+Shift+E** on Windows or **Command+Shift+E** on Mac). In doing so, the Export dialogue box will pop up.

- To begin, choose where you wish to store the exported photos in the Export window. You can choose a new folder or use the one that was originally selected.

- Use the "**File Naming**" section to modify the file name convention. You can use different tokens, such as dates and sequence numbers, to build a custom filename or choose one from a preset.

File Settings:

o **Format**: Select the file type (JPEG, TIFF, PSD, etc.) that you want to use for your exported photos. Because JPEG files are smaller, they are often a good option for online use.

o **Quality**: Modify the JPEG picture quality option. Larger file sizes are associated with greater quality levels, but better picture quality.

o **Color Space**: Make sure you choose the right color space. While Adobe RGB or ProPhoto RGB could be better for printing, sRGB is often used for online usage.

o **Bit Depth**: Select the bit depth that you want for your exported photos. While 16-bit is sometimes used for printing to preserve more color information, 8-bit is the norm on the web.

Image Sizing:

o **Resize to Fit:** If you want to resize the pictures, provide the measurements. You may specify a maximum width or height for web usage. You might adjust the proportions for printing according to the print size.

o **Resolution:** Choose the image resolution. The standard for the web is 72 pixels per inch. Use a higher resolution (such as 300 pixels per inch) for printing.

• **Output Sharpening:** Apply sharpening according to the output medium for output. Select "**Matte**" or "**Glossy**" for print, and

"**Screen**" for the web. To get the required degree of sharpness, adjust the quantity.

- **Metadata**: Select the information you want to attach to your exported photos. This may include keywords, copyright information, and other specifics.

- **Watermarking (Optional):** The Watermarking area is where you may apply a watermark to your photos. Personalize the location and look of the watermark.

- **Post-Processing**: Select the action to take after export. The exported photos may be seen on your file explorer or opened in another program.

- **Presets:** If you anticipate using your export settings often, save them as a preset. When exporting comparable groups of photographs, this may save time.

- **Export**: To begin the export process, click the "**Export**" button once you've adjusted every parameter.

CHAPTER THIRTEEN

Best export settings for high-resolution prints

Make sure you have properly arranged and processed your photographs in Lightroom Classic before exporting.

Select the Appropriate File Format

- o **File Format:** Choose the "**JPEG**" format for the file. Although TIFF is an additional choice, JPEG is more often used and offers a decent trade-off between file size and picture quality.

- o **Quality:** Select the maximum setting (100) on the quality slider. This guarantees optimal picture quality and less compression.

Remember that greater file sizes are the consequence of using higher-quality settings.

Image Sizing

- o Select the "**Resize to Fit**" option by checking the box. This is where you will provide the image's dimensions. It's typically advisable to use the dimensions your print provider recommends or the professional printing standards' resolution recommendations for high-quality prints (usually 300 pixels per inch or higher).

- o **Resolution**: 300 pixels per inch (ppi) should be the resolution setting. The industry standard for fine-art prints is this resolution. Make the necessary adjustments if the print provider or your printer suggests a different resolution.

Output Sharpening

- o **Sharpening**: Use output sharpening that is tailored to printing. **Select "Glossy Paper" or "Matte Paper"** according to the kind of paper you want to print on.

Metadata

- o **Include All Metadata**: Select this option if you want to include data such as camera settings, copyright information, etc. into the exported file.

Watermarking

- o **Watermarking**: You can safeguard your photos by adding a watermark if you'd like. Adjust the watermark's parameters to suit your tastes.

Destination

o **Decide on a Destination**: Pick the folder in which you want to store the exported photos. You have the option of exporting straight to a designated folder or the same folder as the source photos.

o **File Naming**: Modify the file names according to your needs.

Export

o To begin the export process, click the "**Export**" button. After that, Lightroom Classic will process your photos using the chosen parameters and save them in the selected folder.

How to work and install external editors

First of all, verify that your external editor is compatible with Adobe Lightroom Classic before continuing. Affinity Photo, Adobe Photoshop, and other options are popular alternatives.

The steps:

- Launch Lightroom Classic.

- From the top menu bar, choose **Edit (Windows) or Lightroom (Mac).**

- After selecting Preferences, choose **External Editing**.

- Select the preferred file format, which is often TIFF or PSD.

- Choose a color space (Adobe RGB works well for print, sRGB is typical for the web).

- Adjust additional settings, such as Bit Depth and Resolution.

- You have the option to adjust the Resolution to suit your output requirements.

- Choose between editing the original (Edit Original) or a copy of the original (Edit a Copy with Lightroom Adjustments).

- If you want to arrange altered versions, you can also choose the Stack With Original option.

- Select the Additional External Editor option by clicking the Choose button in the External Editing settings.

- Open your external editor's executable file (Photoshop.exe, for example).

- Set the File Naming under External Editing Preferences and choose the folder in which you want to save the altered photos

- Choose a picture from the Library section.

- From the context menu, choose **Edit In** with a right-click.

- Choose the external editor that you set up.

- Using the external editor, make your revisions and save them.

- Return to Lightroom after making any necessary changes to the picture in the external editor and saving them. The original and the modified picture will be available in your library.

- You can keep adjusting, adding information, and organizing your modified photos in Lightroom.

How to understand and use smart collections

Adobe Lightroom Classic's Smart Collections are an effective tool for effectively managing and organizing your picture collection according to predetermined standards. Smart collections, in contrast to normal collections, are dynamic—that is, they automatically add images that satisfy predefined criteria.

Here's how to understand and use smart collections:

- Launch Lightroom Classic.

- Locate the Collections panel on the left side of the Library module. The Smart Collections area is located underneath the standard collections.

- Hold down the mouse pointer above the "**Smart Collections**" heading and choose "**Create Smart Collection.**"

- Proceed to name your smart collection.

- You can choose from a variety of criterion settings in the Smart Collection dialog box, including Keywords, Metadata, Date, Rating, and more.

- Select the settings that best suit your requirements. For instance, you might make a smart collection of images with a certain keyword or within a given period range.

- Adjust your smart collection by adding more rules. To add a rule, click the **"+"** button and choose the rule's criteria. You can now design intricate conditions thanks to this.

- Choose if it is necessary to follow every rule (Match all) or whether it is sufficient to follow only one of the rules (Match any).

- You can also exclude certain standards. Take all the photos that have the term "**Travel**" in them, but leave out the ones that include the phrase "**Work**."

- The smart collection will dynamically display in the Preview area the number of photographs that meet your specified criteria as you configure them. This helps you gauge the size of the collection.

- Choose "**Create**" to save your clever assortment.

Using Smart Collections:

- As you add new images or edit ones that already exist and meet the requirements, smart collections are updated automatically.

- Without physically rearranging your photos, use smart collections to arrange them according to different criteria.

- Make bulk modifications to every picture in a smart collection at the same time. For instance, you may apply a certain preset or change the exposure.

- Smart collections automate the process of arranging and categorizing photographs, which streamlines your productivity.

- To artistically explore your picture library, use smart collections. For example, make a collection of intelligent images that you haven't modified yet but have low ratings.

How to understand and use smart previews

Adobe Lightroom Classic's Smart Previews are an effective tool that lets you edit your pictures even if the actual files aren't accessible. Since they are more portable and compact copies of your raw photos, you can edit them while on the road or while your original files are on an external disk.

- Before working on any picture, you must create a Smart Preview, separate from the actual file. Make sure your catalog is open before creating Smart Previews, then choose the Library module.

- After choosing the photos you want to work with, choose **'Library' > 'Previews' > 'Build Smart Previews.'**

- When the original files are not linked, Lightroom Classic utilizes Smart Previews automatically, letting you edit and organize without requiring the original files.

Using Smart Previews:

- If the original files are not accessible or you detach your external drive, Lightroom Classic will automatically switch to Smart Previews. **(NB: This lets you go on with your editing process without any problems).**

- Using Smart Previews for editing helps improve Lightroom Classic's overall speed, particularly when handling a lot of high-resolution photos.

- Lightroom Classic will automatically use the original files for exporting, guaranteeing the best possible quality in the final exported picture, when you use Smart Previews to export photographs.

- Lightroom Classic instantly reverts to editing with the original files whenever you reconnect the external disk or make the original files accessible.

- Smart Previews are a useful choice if you're working on a laptop or other device with limited storage since they use less space than the actual raw files.

- The Develop module functions the same with Smart Previews as it does with the actual files. But bear in mind that for best effects, certain sophisticated editing functions may need the original file.

Tips for Smart Previews:

- To enable seamless editing even in situations when the original files are unavailable, it's a good idea to create Smart Previews for the photos you're currently working on.

- Even though Smart Previews use less space than actual files, you should still keep an eye on how much data you're using, particularly if your collection is big.

- When using Smart Previews, Lightroom Classic settings may be adjusted to maximize speed. These options are located in the preferences menu.

Lightroom's Integration with Photoshop

For photographers and image editors, Adobe Lightroom Classic and Photoshop are two essential tools. By facilitating a smooth workflow, its integration enables users to fully use the advantages of each software.

Initial Import and Organization:

- Lightroom Classic is often where photographers start the process by importing and organizing their images.

- With its extensive organizing tools, Lightroom Classic lets users add keywords, create collections, and customize metadata for their photos.

Basic Editing in Lightroom:

- Lightroom Classic's non-destructive editing features are well-known. Without changing the original picture data, photographers may edit exposure, contrast, color balance, and other aspects of their images.

- Lightroom Classic's Develop module offers many options for picture adjustment.

Advanced Photoshop Editing:

- Users can easily move their photos from Lightroom Classic to Photoshop when finer or pixel-level processing is needed.

- In Lightroom Classic, this is usually accomplished by selecting an image, simply right-click and choose "**Edit in Adobe Photoshop**".

Photoshop Smart Objects and Non-Destructive Editing:

- Using Smart Objects while transferring photos to Photoshop is part of the integration. The original image data is preserved by Smart Objects, enabling non-destructive manipulation.

- To ensure a synced workflow, adjustments performed in Photoshop are mirrored back in Lightroom Classic.

Round-Trip Editing:

- Once an image has been altered in Photoshop, it is saved, and Lightroom Classic instantly updates with the modified version.

- After editing photos, users can still use Lightroom Classic's categorization and organizing tools.

Sharing and Exporting:

- After finishing the editing process, Lightroom Classic allows photographers to export their photos straight from the program.

- Lightroom Classic offers an array of export options, including file format, size, and quality settings, which facilitate seamless online and print picture sharing.

Cloud Integration (if applicable):

- There may be connectivity with Adobe Creative Cloud for cloud-based photo sharing and storage, depending on the version and Adobe upgrades.

How to use the spot removal tool

A vital step in photo editing is to use Adobe Lightroom Classic 2024's Spot Removal tool to eliminate distracting spots, blemishes, and other imperfections from your images.

Follow the steps below to use the spot removal tool:

- Open Adobe Lightroom Classic and open the image you want to edit.

- Click the "**Develop**" tab located in the upper right corner of the screen to access the Develop module.

- Zoom in on the image. Focus on the area you want to touch up. You can click on the picture by using the "Z" key or by using the Zoom tool.

- Find the "**Spot Removal**" tool in the right-hand panel. It seems to be a pin in a circle.

- Use the slider or the "[" and "]" keys to change the brush's size. The size of the place you want to delete should correspond with the brush size.

- Choose between "**Clone**" and "**Heal.**"
  - **Clone**: Layers a portion of a picture on top of another, duplicating the color and texture of one area.

o **Heal**: Creates a smooth transition between the region around the spot and its surrounding texture and color.

- Click on a nearby area with a comparable texture and color. Lightroom will use this as the source point in line with the spot.

- Lightroom will take care of the spot removal automatically after the source point is placed. You can use the opacity slider or drag the source point to fine-tune the results if necessary.

- Click on each spot separately to keep eliminating them. Lightroom will choose a source point on its own, but you can change it if needed.

- Use the spacebar to navigate around your image as you work on it. This will allow you to access different areas.

- To view a preview of your edits before and after, press the backslash key "". This aids in your assessment of the modifications you've made.

- Make any last tweaks to the exposure, contrast, and color balance of the entire picture.

- After you're satisfied with your edits, you can export your photo or carry out additional processing.

Advanced watermarking techniques

The steps:

- To watermark an image, open **Adobe Lightroom Classic** and import the desired pictures.

- Press 'D' on your keyboard to navigate to the "**Develop**" module within the Library module.

- Navigate to the Develop module's "**Watermarking**" panel on the right.

- To add a new watermark, click the "**Watermark Editor**" button.

- Select a watermark type, either text or graphic.

- Type your text into the designated box to create a text watermark. To alter the look, change the font, size, style, color, and opacity. Additionally, you can add a shadow to improve visibility.

- Click "**Select a Watermark File**" to select the graphic file if one is being used. Modify the graphic's opacity, size, and anchor point.

- To position the watermark, use the anchor points (bottom-right, center, etc.). Use the Offset sliders to fine-tune the position.

- Preset your watermark settings so you can use them again later.

- Look around the Effects panel to add more personalization.

- If you want the watermark to stand out more, you can add effects like a drop shadow or bevel.

- Choose multiple images from the Filmstrip at the bottom to apply the watermark. Select the watermark settings by clicking the "**Sync Settings**" button.

- Select the Export dialog box once the watermark has been applied. Verify that the Export dialog's "**Watermark**" option is selected. If necessary, modify the remaining export parameters and select "**Export**."

- To prevent unauthorized use without drawing attention away from the image, think about adding a faint, semi-transparent watermark. Try out various configurations to determine the ideal ratio of subtlety to visibility.

- Return to the Watermark Editor and change the settings if you need to make adjustments to the watermark.

How to use the HSL panel

With Adobe Lightroom Classic, the HSL panel is an effective tool that lets you fine-tune the colors in your photos. It is an acronym for Hue, Saturation, and Luminance, each of which has three adjustable parameters for different color ranges.

The steps:

- First of all, import your image into Lightroom Classic.

- Select the "**Develop**" module by clicking on it in the upper-right corner of the screen.

- The Develop module has several panels on the right side. The "**HSL / Grayscale**" panel should be visible. To increase its choices, click on it.

- There are three tabs on the HSL panel: **"Hue,"** **"Saturation," and "Luminance."** You can change a certain feature of the colors in your picture with each tab.

- Select the tab labeled "**Hue**". Here, you can change the color of different color ranges. For instance, you can change the image's green tones without changing the other colors.

- Go to the tab labeled "**Saturation**". You have control over the color intensity here. Colors may be desaturated by decreasing the saturation or made more bright by increasing it.

- Select "**Luminance**" from the menu. This gives you the ability to adjust the brightness of certain colors. For example, you can change the sky's blue tones without changing the other colors.

- The Hue, Saturation, and Luminance tabs each include a little symbol that resembles a hand. To make use of the Targeted Adjustment Tool, click on it. Using this tool, you can change the appropriate color by clicking and dragging on a certain region of your picture.

- For finer changes, you can also use the sliders located under each tab in addition to the Targeted Adjustment Tool. Try adjusting these sliders until you get the desired appearance.

- Access the before-and-after view by hitting the "Y" key or by using the backslash key ("") to compare the altered picture with the original as you make changes.

- Export your picture or go on to other editing activities after you're happy with your changes.

CHAPTER FOURTEEN

How to use black-and-white profiles

Follow the steps:

- Open Lightroom Classic and choose your image.

- In the upper-right corner of the screen, choose the "**Develop**" module.

- Before using a black-and-white profile, you may wish to make some minor picture modifications. Adjustments to exposure, contrast, highlights, shadows, and other aspects might be among them.

- Locate the "**Profile Browser**" panel on the right side of the screen in the Develop module.

Usually, it's situated underneath the Basic panel.

- In the Profile Browser panel, choose "**Profile**" from the drop-down menu.

- Choose "**Artistic**" or "**Black & White**" by swiping down. A range of black-and-white profiles from Adobe may significantly alter the appearance of your picture.

- You'll receive a preview of how various profiles will appear when you hover over them. Select the profile that best captures the idea you have for the picture.

- Using the different adjustment sliders in the Develop module, you may further refine your picture after applying a black-and-white profile. Controls for contrast, clarity, and other tonal changes could be among them.

- Use the HSL/Grayscale panel for more exact control over the black-and-white conversion. This lets you change the black-and-white image's brightness for certain hues.

- After making the necessary adjustments, you can save your work or export the picture in the format of your choice.

Tips:

- **Undo/Redo:** To compare various profile configurations, use the keyboard keys for **"Undo" (Ctrl+Z or Command+Z)** and **"Redo" (Shift+Ctrl+Z or Shift+Command+Z).**

- **Presets**: Apply and further tweak the black and white presets that Adobe Lightroom Classic may provide.

How to understand and use the detail panel

One of the most useful tools in Adobe Lightroom Classic is the Detail panel, which lets you sharpen and minimize noise in your images. It is very helpful for adjusting the details in your photos to give them a polished appearance.

The steps:

- Upon launching Adobe Lightroom Classic, choose the **Develop module** by hitting the 'D.'

- The panels are on the right-hand side. Once you reach the "**Detail**" tab, scroll down.

- It's helpful to enlarge the picture to have a better look at the precise regions you want to improve before making any particular adjustments.

- To enlarge the picture, use the Navigator panel or the Zoom tool.

Sharpening:

- o **Amount**: The sharpening's strength is adjusted using this slider. To make it more pointed, move it to the right.

- o **Radius**: Modifies how big the sharpened details become. Greater values have an impact on greater areas, whereas smaller values concentrate on finer details.

- o **Detail**: By highlighting or minimizing the details, this slider adjusts the sharpness. Take caution while using it to prevent adding artifacts.

Noise Reduction:

- o **Luminance**: Manages the decrease in luminance noise or the graininess in color brightness. Raise it to cut down on noise, but watch out not to lose too much information.

o **Color**: Specifically targets color noise. Make adjustments to lessen color speckles without degrading the color's overall quality.

Masking

o You can apply sharpening selectively thanks to this function. To see the regions where sharpness will be applied, move the Masking slider while holding down the **'Alt'** (Option on Mac) key. Avoiding sharpening regions with too little detail is beneficial.

Before and After View:

o To observe the effect of your changes, switch between the before and after views by using the 'Y' key.

- o Alternatively, to get a side-by-side comparison, use the **'Backslash'** key ().

Resetting Adjustments:

- o Double-click the name or value of any slider to return it to its initial state in any panel.

Applying Changes:

- Proceed with more modifications in the Develop module if you're happy with the changes you made in the Detail panel.

- Don't forget to occasionally enlarge the picture to get the full effect.

- Once you've made all the required changes, choose the Library module and save or share your revised picture by using the **Export function**.

- If you find yourself making similar detail tweaks often, you may want to save them as presets for later use.

How to customize and use shortcuts

Changing Adobe Lightroom Classic Shortcuts:

Using Adobe Lightroom Classic's customizable shortcuts can help you work more productively and optimize your productivity.

Access the Keyboard Shortcuts below:

- Turn on your PC and launch Adobe Lightroom Classic.

- Select "**Edit**" from the Windows menu, or "**Lightroom**" from the Mac menu.

- In Windows, choose "**Preferences**"; in Mac, choose "**Lightroom Classic**".

- After selecting the "**Presets**" option, choose "**Show All Other Lightroom Presets.**"

Navigating to the Shortcut Editor:

- Select the "**External Editing**" tab in the Preferences dialog box.

- Locate the area labeled "**Additional External Editor**".

- Select the option labeled "**Choose**" located next to "**Additional External Editor.**"

Customizing Shortcuts:

- There are many options available to you in the External Editing Preset dialog.

- Choose the command you want to modify and click the "**Shortcut**" option.

- Hit the key combination that you want to designate as the shortcut.

- After choosing the shortcuts you want, click "**Done**" or "**Save**" to make the changes effective.

Using Adobe Lightroom Classic Shortcuts:

- Use the built-in help function or consult Adobe's official documentation to get familiar with the default keyboard shortcuts.

- Use the designated shortcuts to carry out different activities. For instance, 'E' for the Loupe view, 'D' for the Develop module, and 'G' for the Grid view.

- Certain shortcuts function only in certain modules or views. Investigate the shortcuts that apply to the work you're doing.

- Should you discover that certain built-in shortcuts aren't appropriate for your work process, return to the Preferences window and make the necessary adjustments.

- Try out several shortcuts to see which one suits you the best. To create muscle memory, practice utilizing them often.

- The "**Restore All Defaults**" option in the Preferences window allows you to go back to the original shortcut configurations at any time.

How to create and use synchronized settings

In Adobe Lightroom Classic, synchronized settings are created and used by applying changes made to one picture to many chosen photographs. This is especially helpful if you want to apply the same settings to all of the photographs in a series that were shot under comparable circumstances.

Using and Creating Synchronized Lightroom Classic Settings:

- Launch Adobe Lightroom Classic, then import the desired images for editing.

- Click the "**Develop**" tab located in the upper right corner of the screen to get to the Develop module.

- Select one picture, then use the Develop module to make the necessary changes. This can include adjusting the white balance, contrast, exposure, and so on.

- After editing the first picture, go to the Develop module's left side. The "**Sync**" button is located at the bottom. Ensure you select it.

- A list of all the settings you may sync will be shown in a dialog box that opens. Select the settings (such as Basic Tone, White Balance, Tone Curve, etc.) that you want to synchronize. Syncing cropping, spot removal, and local tweaks are further options.

- Click "**Synchronize**" after the required parameters have been chosen.

- Go to the Library module now.

- Choose the pictures that you want to use the same settings for. To pick several photos, use Ctrl (Windows) or Command (Mac).

- From the context menu that appears when you right-click on one of the chosen images, choose "**Develop Settings**" and then "**Sync Settings**."

- You'll be prompted with a dialog box to approve the synchronization. Check the settings you want to synchronize, then choose "**Synchronize**."

- Examine the synchronized images and make any required changes. Different lighting circumstances may call for different modifications for each shot.

- After you're OK with the synchronized settings, you may export the pictures or keep adjusting each one as you see fit.

- If you want the settings to be used while viewing the photos in other programs, don't forget to save the metadata modifications.

How to understand profiles in digital camera

The steps:

- Import your images into Adobe Lightroom Classic. After the import is successful, they appear in the Library module.

- Click the "Develop" tab in the upper-right corner of the screen to get to the Develop module. You'll do most of your editing work here.

- After that, locate the "**Camera Calibration**" tab by swiping right. Usually, it's found toward the bottom of the panel on the right.

- You can choose from a variety of camera profiles using the "**Profile**" dropdown menu found in the Camera Calibration panel. The

Adobe Standard profile is often used by default in Adobe Lightroom Classic, although you may choose additional profiles to get distinct styles.

- To see the various profiles, choose the Profile option from the dropdown menu. Options like Adobe Color, Adobe Monochrome, Adobe Landscape, and so forth could be available. Every profile gives your picture a unique interpretation in terms of color and tone. Try a variety of profiles and see how they impact your reputation.

- Use creative profiles in Adobe Lightroom Classic in addition to the pre-installed ones to give your images a particular look or feel. Creative profiles are often called after cinema or photography genres. To examine and use imaginative profiles, choose the "**Browse**" option from the Profile dropdown menu.

- Change the "**Amount**" slider to fine-tune the effect of a profile on your picture once you've chosen one. This regulates how strong the profile impact is. To fine-tune the effect on little details in your picture, you may also use the "**Detail**" slider.

- Click the "+" symbol next to the Profile dropdown if you've made particular changes to a profile and would want to store it for later use. This enables you to put up your favorite camera profile settings in a custom one.

- You can switch between your image's before and after views by using the backslash key ("") to see the effect of your selected profile. This enables you to assess the modifications made by the profile and modify the settings as necessary.

- After choosing a camera profile, proceed with your standard editing process, modifying exposure, contrast, color balance, and other settings to get the desired effect for your image.

- Once your editing is complete, click the "**Export**" button located in the bottom-left corner of the screen to export your picture.

How to manage color accuracy in

Lightroom Classic 2024

Controlling color accuracy in Adobe Lightroom Classic is essential to producing consistent and eye-catching picture editing outcomes.

- Use a hardware calibration tool to begin by calibrating your display. This guarantees the accuracy of the colors you see on your screen. X-Rite ColorMunki and Datacolor Spyder are two well-liked tools.

- Select **"Lightroom Classic" > "Preferences" (Mac) or "Edit" > "Preferences" (Windows).**

- Select the **"External Editing"** option in the Preferences box.

- Choose between Adobe RGB and ProPhoto RGB for the **"Color Space"**; Adobe RGB is a fine option for most uses, while ProPhoto RGB has a broader gamut.

- Upon importing images, go to the Library section.

- Select the **"Apply During Import"** tab in the Import dialog box to **"Develop Settings"** and select a preset or custom settings based on your preferred color scheme.

Develop Module Adjustments:

- Move to the Develop Module.

- To fix any color casts in your photos, use the Basic panel to change the Temperature and Tint settings.

- Keep an eye on the Histogram to make sure the distribution of tones is equal.

Profile Corrections:

- Locate the "**Lens Corrections**" panel in the Develop module.

- Turn on "**Enable Profile Corrections**" to fix chromatic aberration and lens distortion.

Soft Proofing:

- To see how your photo will appear printed, use the Soft Proofing option.

- Select the relevant printer profile in the Develop section and use the S key to activate Soft Proofing.

HSL/Color Panel:

- Adjust individual colors in your picture by using the HSL/Color panel.

- Modify each color's hue, saturation, and luminance to get the desired effect.

RGB Values:

- While making changes, pay attention to the RGB values in the histogram. This makes sure you don't lose detail by cutting any channels.

Export Settings:

- Make sure you choose the right color space before exporting. If the majority of your photos will be used online, stay with sRGB.

- Modify the export parameters to correspond with the picture's planned use, whether it is online, in print, or for another reason.

- Make sure your color management process satisfies your current requirements by reviewing it regularly.

- Keep up with any updates to Adobe Lightroom Classic that might improve color management.

How to set up and use Lightroom Classic with an External Monitor or Dual Monitor

An additional monitor, or two, may greatly improve your productivity while using Lightroom Classic by giving you more screen real estate for tools, previews, and an immersive editing experience. To set up two displays or easily incorporate an external monitor with Adobe Lightroom Classic 2024, follow these steps:

Connect External Monitor(s):

- Verify that your PC can accommodate many displays. The majority of contemporary PCs support HDMI, DisplayPort, or USB-C connections to external monitors.

- Attach your external monitor to the computer's corresponding port.

- Use the available port to connect the second monitor in a twin monitor setup.

Examine the Graphics Preferences:

- To access "**Display settings**" on Windows or "**System Settings**" > "**Displays**" on Mac, do a right-click on the desktop.

- Verify that the system has identified both monitors and that they are positioned as needed. If necessary, change the angle and resolution.

Continued steps:

- Turn on your PC and launch Adobe Lightroom Classic 2024.

- Select "**Edit**" from the top menu (Windows) or "**Lightroom Classic**" (Mac).

- Select "**Preferences**" using the menu drop-down.

- Select the "**Performance**" tab in the Preferences dialog box.

- Locate and confirm that the "**Use Graphics Processor**" option is activated.

- Select "**Use Smart Previews Instead of Originals for image editing**" by checking the box.

- To use your external monitor, choose the "**Use Additional Display**" selection option.

- Select the "**Window**" option if you're utilizing two monitors.

- To use the second monitor, choose **"Secondary Display"** and then **"Loupe," "Grid," or "Compare."** Tailor each monitor's view to your tastes.

- To optimize the workspace, drag Lightroom's main window across both displays.

- Panels can be resized or moved across displays to create an effective arrangement.

- Select "**Solo Mode**" with a right-click on the module selector to concentrate on only one module at a time.

- Click "OK" to preserve your settings for your external monitor or dual displays in the Preferences dialog box.

- Import your images into Lightroom Classic and begin editing.

- To improve workflow efficiency, make use of the extra screen real estate by keeping your tools, histograms, and previews displayed at the same time.

- Check that the displays are calibrated to provide precise color reproduction. For accurate color reproduction, which is essential for picture editing, use a calibration tool.

- Be sure you save your work after editing, and when you're ready to export, compare the photos across the two displays to be sure they're consistent.

Troubleshooting Common Lightroom Classic Issues

Lightroom Classic is a great software for editing, however, like any program, however, it may have problems that interfere with your productivity.

Slow Performance:

Lightroom Classic is operating slowly, which makes it difficult to work effectively.

Troubleshooting Steps:

- **Optimize Catalog**: To improve speed, optimize your catalog regularly. Select Optimize Catalog under Library.

- **Preview Generation**: Performance may be impacted by previews. When zooming in, generate 1:1 previews to speed up rendering.

- Hardware Acceleration: Navigate to **Preferences > Performance** and check your GPU settings. Enhancing performance may be greatly increased by turning on GPU acceleration.

Corrupt Catalog

Photos may disappear or there may be mistakes in the catalog due to corruption.

Troubleshooting steps:

- **Backup Catalog:** To prevent data loss, regularly backup your catalog. Make use of **File > Export as Catalog** to make a copy.

- To confirm the catalog, choose **File > Optimize Catalog**. Certain catalog problems may be found and resolved using this procedure.

Importing Issues

Either photos cannot be imported or photos are not shown after they are.

Troubleshooting steps:

- **Verify the Source**: Make sure the source disk or folder is usable and undamaged.

- **Destination Drive**: Verify that the drive has enough space.

- **File formats:** Make sure Lightroom can import the file formats you're attempting to import.

Develop Module Errors:

Problem: The Develop module crashes or produces errors when used.

Troubleshooting steps:

- **Update GPU Drivers:** Make sure the drivers for your graphics card are current.

- To reset the develop settings, right-click a picture, choose **Develop Settings**, then select **Reset**.

- **Isolate the Issue:** To determine whether the issue still exists, try making modifications to a different picture or starting a new catalog.

Missing Images:

Problem: There are missing or exclamation point-filled photos.

Troubleshooting issues:

- **Locate Missing Folder**: In the Library module, right-click on a missing folder and choose "**Find Missing Folder.**"

- **Examine External Drives:** Verify that external drives that contain images are connected.

Freezes and Crashes:

Problem: Lightroom Classic freezes or crashes without warning.

Troubleshooting steps:

- **Verify System Requirements:** Make sure your setup satisfies the suggested specs provided by Adobe.

- **Update Lightroom:** Make sure you're running Lightroom Classic on the most recent version.

- **Turn off third-party plugins**: There may be issues with certain plugins. Turn them off and see whether the problem still exists.

Sync Issues with Lightroom Cloud:

Problem: Lightroom Classic and Lightroom Cloud synchronization issues.

Troubleshooting steps:

- **Verify Internet Connection**: Make sure your internet connection is reliable.

- **Verify Sync Status**: To verify the sync status, click the cloud symbol. Fix any sync issues.

Brush and Graduated Filters Problems:

Problem: Gradient filters or brushes aren't performing as they should.

Troubleshooting steps:

- To reset all of your tools, right-click on the Brush or Graduated Filter tool icon and choose **"Reset All Tools."**

- **Adjust Opacity and Flow:** Verify the brushes' opacity and flow parameters. For the intended result, adjust them as necessary.

Exporting Issues:

Problem: Mistakes or problems with exporting images.

Troubleshooting steps:

- **Verify Export Settings**: Make sure the file type, quality, and destination are all set correctly.

- **Export in Steps:** When exporting many images, consider doing so in smaller batches.

Keywording and Metadata:

Problem: No keywords or metadata are applied or interpreted.

Troubleshooting steps:

- **Examine the Metadata Panel**: Ensure that the metadata panel is shown and that you are appropriately applying keywords.

- **Catalog Corruption Check**: To identify and address such problems, use the catalog optimization procedure.

Color Profile Mismatch:

Problem: Compared to other apps, Lightroom's color rendition is different.

Troubleshooting steps:

- **Color Settings:** Verify the color profile settings in your operating system and Lightroom. Be sure they line up.

- **Soft Proofing:** To see an image of how colors would appear printed, use the soft proofing function (**View > Soft Proofing**).

Library Module Thumbnails:

Problem: The Library module's thumbnails are either not loading at all or are showing improperly.

Troubleshooting steps:

- **Preview Quality**: Go to **Library > Previews > Render Standard-Sized Previews** to change the preview quality of the Library module.

- To ensure that thumbnails are checked, right-click on a picture and choose **"Library > Build Standard-Sized Previews."**

Map and GPS Problems:

Problem: Maps are not loading or GPS coordinates are not synchronizing.

Troubleshooting steps:

- **Metadata Panel**: Verify that the metadata panel has the GPS data.

- **Internet Connection:** Verify that your connection to the internet is steady enough to load maps.

White Balance Issues:

Problem: Modifications to the white balance aren't yielding the expected outcomes.

Troubleshooting issues:

- **Auto White Balance**: Toggle between manually adjusting the temperature and tint sliders and using the auto white balance option.

- Reset the Develop Settings: Select **Develop Settings > Reset** with a right-click on the picture.

Watermarking issues:

Problem: When exporting, watermarks are not applied appropriately.

Troubleshooting issues:

- **Verify Watermark Settings**: Make sure the Export dialog's watermark settings are set appropriately.

- If you're using a watermark template, be sure you update it to reflect any changes.

CONCLUSION

Adobe Lightroom Classic 2024 is the newest version released for video and image editors around the world. The software, in recent years, boasts of having millions of users worldwide, and with so many amazing capabilities at its disposal, it is well worth the hype. Purchasing the software allows customers to make use of a plethora of functions, choices, settings, presets, advantages, and much more in addition to its thrilling characteristics.

Users can import pictures, cure red-eye, remove stains, build numerous catalogs, combine catalogs, access catalogs, set up tethering, and more using Lightroom Classic. As a result, these features have been shown to put you on the correct path to learning all there is to know about Lightroom Classic and to practice using its features and functionalities in front of a larger audience.

To start using Lightroom Classic, you also need the appropriate resources, most notably your PC or other device. It will be challenging to discover Lightroom Classic's hidden features and advantages without a Windows or Mac computer.

ABOUT THE AUTHOR

Ernest Woodruff is an American-born tech expert and has bagged a series of praises and acknowledgements for his selfless service to the technology world. His determination and drive for a better tech world has led to his tech writings and blogs. His commitment is also being applauded in the books he has written so far. His notable achievements have been acknowledged by other top technological experts in other countries. With the technological world gradually improving and advancing by the day, the American-born tech expert is sure to leave more legacies for the living and the unborn ones.

Made in United States
Troutdale, OR
11/15/2024

24835581R00199